WHAT'S NEXT?

WHAT'S NEXT?

**THE JOURNEY TO
KNOW GOD, FIND FREEDOM,
DISCOVER PURPOSE,
& MAKE A DIFFERENCE**

Chris Hodges

NELSON
BOOKS

An Imprint of Thomas Nelson

Published in Nashville, Tennessee, by Nelson Books, an imprint of Thomas Nelson. Nelson Books and Thomas Nelson are registered trademarks of HarperCollins Christian Publishing, Inc.

Published in association with Yates & Yates, www.yates2.com.

Thomas Nelson titles may be purchased in bulk for educational, business, fund-raising, or sales promotional use. For information, please e-mail SpecialMarkets@ThomasNelson.com.

ISBN 978-0-7180-9157-6 (eBook)
ISBN 978-0-7180-9156-9 (HC)

Library of Congress Control Number: 2018964305

Printed in the United States of America

19 20 21 22 23 LSC 10 9 8 7 6 5 4 3 2 1

To Larry Stockstill, my pastor
for over thirty-five years.
No one is more responsible for helping
me know God, find freedom, discover
purpose, and make a difference than
you. I am so grateful for my spiritual
heritage. And now I pass on what was
invested in me to future generations.

CONTENTS

CONTENTS

FOREWORD

GET READY—GET SET—GROW!

Chris Hodges is my friend. He is about to become your friend too! A best friend is one who brings out the best in you. He will certainly do that with this book!

The only guarantee that tomorrow is going to get better is if you are growing today. And the most important growth for you and me is our spiritual growth, our walk with God. *What's Next?* is your guide to spiritual growth. Chris Hodges has helped tens of thousands become successful on their spiritual journeys, He's about to help you too!

I have some questions for you. Check the box that interests you right now. Would you like to

- Know God?
- Find Freedom?

- Discover Your Purpose?
- Make a Difference?

I bet you said yes to all four of those questions. I did! If you and I could discover the answers to those four questions and apply those answers to our lives, we would certainly be fulfilled. My excitement for you is increasing right now. Why? Because you are about to start your spiritual growth journey. As you turn the pages of this book you will keep asking yourself . . . *"What's Next?"*

Let me give you a preview of what you will learn in this book. The discoveries start out with a bang!

- God wants to know you.
- God isn't fair, and it's to your advantage.
- Prayer is an ongoing conversation with God.
- When you read the Bible, the Bible reads you.
- Jesus came to earth to give you freedom.
- Positive change happens with positive relationships.
- God doesn't expect perfection from you. He wants honesty.

Okay, let's stop for a moment. Look at all the good things you are already discovering about God and you. I have taken this same journey that you are now on. And guess what? As you keep walking, the journey gets better. Here are some of my favorite parts of what is coming in the following pages:

- You were created on purpose, for a purpose.
- When you discover your purpose you will say, "I was born for this."
- Your spiritual growth is dependent on having a church family.
- Learn how to live out the healthy four-step growth plan.
- Discover the twelve questions you need to ask yourself regularly in order to thrive.
- Learn how to serve God and others.
- Learn how to live beyond your life.
- Discover the key to changing your world.
- And—this is my favorite part of the book—you will learn to identify a dream from God and see how to make it come true!

Wow! What a book! Read it. Reflect on it. Share what you are learning from it. And, most importantly, apply it every day to your life. Your spiritual growth should be a top priority in your life. To assist you in making this journey a top priority, please apply these Laws of Growth to your daily habits:

- **Law of Intentionality—growth doesn't just happen.** Take some time every day—even for a few minutes—to read this book.
- **Law of the Mirror—you must see value in yourself to add value to yourself.** Understand that pursuing

growth is important and reading this book will daily add value to your life and improve your self-worth.

- **Law of Modeling—it's hard to improve when you have no one but yourself to follow.** *What's Next?* will become your mentor and guide to a better life.
- **Law of Contribution—growing yourself enables you to grow others.** Study this book with a friend or small group.

Let's get started, my friend. Let's see *"what's next"* for you. Today is the first day of the rest of your life. It's about to get better!

—John C. Maxwell, *New York Times* bestselling author

INTRODUCTION

BEFORE YOU BEGIN

Getting lost in Italy sounds a lot more romantic than it actually is. I know this firsthand from when I took my wife, Tammy, on a much-anticipated, long-saved-up-for trip to the booted peninsula to mark a milestone wedding anniversary. We had carefully planned our itinerary, flying into Rome and spending a few days there before heading to a small village in the beautiful region of Tuscany. From there we would travel north to places we had always dreamed of seeing: Florence, Venice, and Lake Como.

After spending a few amazing days in Rome, we understood why it is called the Eternal City. History saturates the ancient capital, and we marveled at iconic places, such as the Colosseum, the Arch of Titus, the Roman Forum, and Palatine Hill, and other sites mentioned by

Paul in Acts and Romans. Leaving Rome, we hired a driver to take us to the rural area in Tuscany, famous for its vineyards and olive groves, where we would be staying. Although we didn't have the specific address of our hotel, our driver, an older Italian gentleman with silver hair and a confident smile, assured us he knew how to get there.

As we crawled through the urban sprawl of Rome, our driver deftly managed the Italian highway system. Tammy and I oohed and aahed over the beautiful Italian countryside as we turned off the main highway onto a country road that took us into the hilly farmland. After an hour of driving, we saw fewer and fewer cars and more bicycles, horses, and sheep as the lush green hillsides displayed terraces of grape vineyards, fig trees, and olive groves. I asked our driver how much longer until we arrived at our destination, but he simply said, "Soon," and smiled back at us.

About that time, I realized he wasn't using a GPS, as there wasn't any kind of electronic navigational tool on the car dash. I didn't see a smart phone anywhere near him either. Feeling a little concerned, I brought up our hotel's name on my own phone only to discover I had no reception. We were deep in the Italian countryside, and with each passing kilometer, my confidence in our driver's knowledge of the area faded.

After a few more minutes, we saw what appeared to be a village around the next curve. When our driver slowed and brought the car to a stop in front of an *osteria*, a quaint little rustic restaurant, Tammy and I breathed a sigh of relief and assumed we had reached our destination. But then our driver said, "Let me get my bearings before we continue on." While we waited, and our driver studied a map so old it might have belonged to the apostle Paul, Tammy discovered her phone had a signal and pulled up our location on a satellite map. We were nowhere close to where we wanted to go. When I tried to show our driver, he simply shook his head, and said, "No worry, my friend, I know how to get there."

He started driving again, but after a few minutes it was clear that we were backtracking and returning the way we had come. Tammy's phone maintained its signal, and when we typed in the name of our hotel, the female voice of the GPS announced, "You have reached your destination." Looking around at more fields dotted with red poppies and tall cedar trees, we could only laugh. Once again, we were in the hands of our driver and his ability to navigate.

"Let's go back to that last village," I said to the driver. "We can ask someone there how to get to our location."

He nodded but continued driving in the same direction.

Annoyed that he apparently ignored my suggestion, I wasn't sure what else we could do but continue on and hope our driver eventually stumbled across our destination.

Sensing my frustration, Tammy said, "When you were growing up, did your family ever get lost while taking a road trip? It seemed to happen every summer with my family. I remember how my mom would get so mad at

Dad because he'd never stop to ask directions. He'd just study his little Rand McNally map some more and keep trying, usually until all of us were starving and so tired we couldn't keep our eyes open."

I laughed. "Oh yes, I remember those good old days. My daddy was the same way. You know how we are as guys," I said, nodding toward our friend in the driver's seat, "about not asking for help or admitting we can't figure something out on our own. Thank goodness for GPS."

"If only we had GPS," Tammy said.

The afternoon light was beginning to fade. We saw no other signs of life anywhere. Getting frustrated, I studied the map on my phone, annoyed that technology wasn't working like it should, and once again tried to talk to our driver. More and more, I felt like we were driving in circles, making the same ten-kilometer loop through the heart of Tuscany.

We knew where we wanted to go.

We thought we had the right directions.

We assumed our tools of technology would work.

We even had a driver with knowledge of the area.

But we were lost.

LOST AND FOUND

With the usually reliable advantage of technology and GPS, I know most people don't get lost very often, but as Tammy and I found out the hard way, it can still happen. (You'll be happy to know our driver eventually managed to get us there—a direct result, I'm convinced, of the prayers Tammy and I eventually began to offer from the backseat!)

When was the last time you got lost? Maybe you were driving to an unfamiliar destination or walking through a foreign city. You might have forgotten your phone or thought you knew where you were going. Or perhaps you couldn't get a phone or wi-fi signal even though your GPS knew the way.

Unfortunately, we all get lost—if not physically and geographically, then spiritually and emotionally. We reach a juncture where we don't know which way to go. A job offer, an opportunity to move, a new relationship, a sense of God's calling—any one of these may be the catalyst, but following through without knowing exactly where your new path will lead can be both exciting and frightening.

As a pastor I get to be a student of people and how they navigate life's path. I encounter so many who don't know where they're going or even where they want to go. They know something is missing, and they long for a clearer sense of purpose and direction, but they just can't seem to find it.

Others have been on a spiritual journey at a comfortable pace for most of their lives—so comfortable, in fact, that they feel caught in a rut, spinning their wheels in a life that feels predictable, even boring. They, too, long for a deeper meaning, a deeper joy, a deeper connection to the God they love and the Savior they're committed to following. But they don't know where to turn or how to step off the treadmill they're on.

Some people are simply exhausted. Perhaps a major detour has left them reeling—a health crisis, divorce, or job loss has rerouted them from the path they once thought their lives would follow. They know God has a plan for them and have caught glimpses of where they're going. But after being sidelined, they're tired and not sure how to get going again.

It may seem like a cliché, but it's true—we're all on a journey. You may have no clue where you are on your journey through life right now, or you might think you know exactly where you are and where you're going. Or, like most of us, you may be somewhere in between: trying to listen to God's voice while watching the road signs, anticipating changes in the weather, and hoping for clear direction at major crossroads.

At various points along our life's journey, we all ask, "Now what? Which way do I go? Which direction is the right direction? Where will this road take me? Is that really where I want to go?" During these crossroads moments, we need to pause and remember our priorities. We need to look beyond what's logical or convenient or advantageous. We need to look to God as our ultimate GPS, our soul's true compass, if we want to live a life that's purposeful, joyful, and significant for eternity.

When we don't see God's vision for our lives, we're in danger of settling for an earthly counterfeit of fulfillment. Without God showing us what's next and leading the way, we tend to focus on ourselves. The emphasis becomes improving ourselves, achieving fame or popularity, building a platform to get our name out there, or making another dollar. But if we want to move forward with true confidence, purpose, and hope, we have to let God guide us.

That's why I've written this book. Not that I've got it all figured out, but I know the One who does—and you can know him too. If your faith journey is just beginning, don't worry, because you won't get lost in these pages. If you're a mature believer who's been walking with Christ for a while now, there's still plenty for you. No matter where you are, let this book be a spiritual field guide to help you find your way.

No matter where you are, you can know what's next!

SECTION 1

KNOW GOD

'll never forget that place.

Even now, decades later, I vividly recall how different it felt: a bit scary yet appealing at the same time, bigger than me but personally inviting as well. I was fifteen and had agreed to visit a friend's church after he told me a lot of girls our age would be there. Not the best of motives, I admit, but at least it got me there.

Church was nothing new to me. I'd grown up in a formal denominational church. I was familiar with liturgy and loved being part of a community filled with my family and friends. As long as I could remember, I had always loved church. But what I realized that day while visiting my buddy's church was that I didn't love God—because I didn't really know him. Basically, I had been going to church to try to earn my way to God.

This church was different from anything I had experienced before. While the pews and pulpit looked about the same, and the hymns and Bibles were also the same, something electric and alive, invisible but tangibly present, charged the atmosphere. There was real passion in the congregation's worship. The preaching was good, but it was the congregation's response that stood out. Other young people were taking notes and highlighting their

Bibles, fully engaged and nodding in agreement with the pastor. Adults did the same, punctuating their attention with an occasional "Amen!" or "That's good!"

This was not what I was used to experiencing on Sunday mornings, let alone the Sunday evening service. But these people made the Christian faith attractive. They had something I didn't, something I wanted. The message pierced my heart that night in a way no other preaching had touched me before. So many thoughts and feelings swirled around inside me. *What is going on here? Is my church teaching the right way to know God? Or is this church? And what is the difference? More importantly, what is the right way?*

I went home that cold December night determined to find the answers, determined to pursue God the way he wanted, even if it wasn't the way I had been taught. I closed the door to my room, plopped down on the shag carpeting at the foot of my bed, and began to think. I knew enough to realize that I couldn't just trust what someone else said or how I felt in this new church or my old one. There had to be a better, more definitive source.

Fortunately, I knew the Bible well enough—one good thing about my church's approach—that I quickly saw it was the only authority I could trust for the ultimate truth about how to know God. The answers had to be in God's Word. That's why God gave it to us, right? As familiar as it was, though, the Bible still seemed so big, so intimidating. Where to begin? The answers were probably there, but how was I supposed to find them?

I started with the words of Jesus himself. It made sense to me that Jesus had people around him in his day asking the same basic question I was asking: *How do I know God?* Fortunately, I had one of those classic red-letter editions of the Bible with the words of Christ printed in bright crimson in contrast to the rest of the black-and-white text. Surely that red ink had been used for such a moment as mine!

Skipping through the Old Testament, I nervously turned those thin, almost tissue-like pages until I began to see words and phrases printed in red. I was only a couple of pages into Matthew when one passage in particular jumped out at me:

> "Not everyone who says to me, 'Lord, Lord,' will enter the kingdom of heaven, but only the one who does the will of my Father who is in heaven. Many will say to me on that day, 'Lord, Lord, did we not prophesy in your name and in your name drive out demons and perform many miracles?' Then I will tell them plainly, 'I never knew you.'" (Matthew 7:21–23)

That passage sent chills down my spine.

It seemed to describe me perfectly, because I had spent my whole life calling him "Lord" for no other reason than that's what everyone told me to do. I had confessed with my mouth that I wanted to be saved, but something crucial was missing. I had never surrendered my heart. I had invited God to come inside but had left the door locked.

That night I realized the truth for the first time. God wasn't looking for my religious actions or waiting for me to attend the correct church. He never wanted me to do things for him to earn his love and forgiveness and grace. He wanted to know me.

I quickly hit rewind on fifteen years of perfect church attendance in my memory. All the Sunday school classes, Scripture memorization, choir rehearsals, Bible studies, prayer meetings, and worship services—I had been part of those all my life, yet I still did not know God personally. Tears welled in my eyes, and my heart drummed so fast I thought it might burst through my chest. I got on my knees and threw my arms over my bed in surrender.

"If you'll give me another chance, Lord, I'll love you," I said. "I want to know you. Really know you."

Something extraordinary happened then; some kind of spiritual ignition fired within me. I fell in love with God. I felt the presence of his Spirit within me. In that moment he became more than the God I had read about or the Creator of the universe. He became my Friend, my Savior, my heavenly Father, my Daddy. He became mine.

KNOWING AND BEING KNOWN

Fast-forward almost forty years later, and I find myself standing in front of people several times a week telling them about this God I know and his love for them. About his Son, Jesus, and the gift of salvation. About the Holy Spirit who wants to empower them and guide them. And what I've realized is that a lot of people are like I was on that cold Sunday night so long ago. They aren't looking for church or religion, for good preaching or a friendly small group. They want to know God.

Now that I've graduated with degrees from Bible school where I studied the original languages of Scripture, I understand that the word Jesus used for "know" in that passage that jumped out at me from Matthew is an intimate term. The Greek word, *genosko*, goes beyond intellectual knowledge or mental awareness to imply personal, firsthand experience. It's the difference between "I know who the mayor is, but I've never met him," and "I know who the mayor is, and he's my best friend."

This kind of knowing is personal and relational, familiar and deeply connected. It's the kind of intimacy we usually associate with marriage. In fact, the Hebrew equivalent that we often translate as "know" refers to the way a woman knows a man before she conceives a child. The word's emphasis is not on the physical, sexual dimension of knowing and being known so much as on the way two people are connected and bound together spiritually.

Why is this important? Because God is the only one who can know you at your deepest levels. He made you and knows the purpose for which you were designed. He alone holds the book on your life and knows the number of your days. You can never find fulfillment and true, lasting joy apart from knowing him. You cannot begin to know what step to take next in your life without him.

Knowing God is the key to life.

And that's what this first section is all about. It's not only the first step in your spiritual journey, but a recurring process of walking with God throughout your life. If you marry someone, your marriage doesn't end after the ceremony or on your first, second, tenth, or golden wedding anniversary. It's an ongoing dynamic relationship, a process of continuing to know each other longer and deeper, closer and closer.

Knowing God is quite similar. You can know his voice by praying, talking, and listening to him. You can know his ways by reading, studying, and applying them.

Maybe as you read these words, you're realizing you don't really know God personally. Like me, you might have grown up in the church and spent your entire life learning about God without ever knowing God. You have all kinds of knowledge and have served your church, but you've never felt intimately close to God. Or maybe you've never been very religious or had a positive experience with the churches you've encountered. But something still draws you, compels you, pulls at your heart to open yourself and give God a chance to enter your life and transform you with his love. Maybe that's the prayer on your lips right now. Wherever you are, whatever you're going through, the fuel for your spiritual journey comes from a real, dynamic, personal, close relationship with the living God.

SURRENDER TO LOVE

Before we can dive into building a deeper relationship with God, we first must establish the foundation for that relationship. Whether you're willing to open your heart to God for the first time or ready for revival and a fresh encounter with the Holy Spirit, knowing God is founded on the simple but crucial understanding that he loves you. You may have memorized this truth or seen it on posters or billboards at ball games, but nothing sums it up better than John 3:16: "For God so loved the world that he gave his one and only Son, that whoever believes in him shall not perish but have eternal life."

Next, out of his immense love for you, God has a unique plan for your life. He wants you to experience the excitement, joy, and contentment that come from doing all that he created you to do. Jesus said, "I have come that they may have life, and have it to the full" (10:10).

If God loves you and wants you to enjoy an abundant life, then why do you feel lonely, disappointed, afraid, and angry so much of the time? Why is it that so many people are not experiencing the abundant life? Simply put, because there is a big problem. We're separated from

God by our inherent sinful nature: "For all have sinned and fall short of the glory of God" (Romans 3:23).

God is holy, and we are not. Our sin—our selfish tendency to always want what we want, when we want it, the way we want it—gets in the way. Left to our own devices and desires, we prevent ourselves from knowing God and experiencing the fullness of the abundant life he wants to give us. Our sinfulness results in death, but God wants us to have eternal life with him. We can't close this gap or change our sinful condition with good works or good intentions. There's only one way: through Jesus Christ. God loves us so much that he sent his Son to die for us and overcome our sin once and for all. "For the wages of sin is death, but the gift of God is eternal life in Christ Jesus our Lord" (6:23).

So often people tell me, "God isn't fair!" And I tell them that I agree with them—God *isn't* fair, and, boy, am I glad he isn't! The truth is we don't deserve anything good—including heaven. We went our own way, and bad things happened as a result. God didn't abandon us, though, and instead sent Jesus on a rescue mission. "God demonstrates His own love toward us, in that while we were still sinners, Christ died for us" (5:8 NKJV). That's why this gift is called "salvation." We're saved from what we deserve and given the gift of new life—an eternal life we could never provide for ourselves. Thank goodness God isn't fair!

If God were fair, then you and I would have to pay for

our sins ourselves, which we can't do! We don't get what we deserve—we get new life, good gifts and abundant blessings, and eternal life with the God who loves us as his children. He was the only one who could take care of our sin problem and the only one to offer the solution. Which explains why Jesus said, "I am the way and the truth and the life. No one comes to the Father except through me" (John 14:6). He was the only one qualified to help us, because he didn't have his own sin. He took on our debt of sin and paid it in full. "Salvation is found in no one else, for there is no other name under heaven given to mankind by which we must be saved" (Acts 4:12).

This gift of salvation requires a response, however. As with any gift, we can choose to accept it, or we can leave it unopened and unreceived. So, there's a choice to be made, a commitment to be determined. "But to all who believed him and accepted him, he gave the right to become children of God" (John 1:12 NLT).

God's Word doesn't stop there in explaining what we must do to accept and activate this gift. How do we believe and accept Jesus into our hearts and lives? The Bible tells us, "If you declare with your mouth, 'Jesus is Lord,' and believe in your heart that God raised him from the dead, you will be saved. For it is with your heart that you believe and are justified, and it is with your mouth that you profess your faith and are saved" (Romans 10:9–10).

If you're reading these words right now, I believe God

is dealing with you. He's speaking to your heart, pursuing you, wooing you, gently and persistently knocking on your door and waiting for your response. "Behold, I stand at the door and knock. If anyone hears My voice and opens the door, I will come in to him" (Revelation 3:20 NKJV). If you're already in a relationship with God and have opened your heart to Jesus, then it's time to find out what's next on your journey; it's time to experience the joy, peace, and purpose you can know as you grow in your faith.

Do you want to know God? Or to grow deeper in love with him?

He wants to know you—deeply and intimately.

Surrender to his love.

Whether for the first time or the eighty-first, give Jesus all areas of your life.

Then you can discover what's next on your incredible spiritual journey!

CHAPTER ONE

BAPTISM

THE WEDDING BAND
OF CHRISTIANITY

I was so excited. The girl I had searched for my whole life was getting ready to be my wife. Now, more than three decades later, I can't think about that day without smiling and feeling exceedingly grateful. Next to my relationship with God, my relationship with Tammy remains my most important connection. Marrying Tammy is still one of the best decisions I ever made.

I had dated quite a bit growing up—I'll save those stories and regrets for another book—but I did learn something. Dating relationships can be close, but, ultimately, they're not committed. Each person has an escape hatch that allows them to keep their options open. At any time, either one can change their mind.

Marriage, on the other hand (the left hand with the ring on it!), is different. It closes that escape hatch and excludes all other options. When you marry, you're making a vow that declares, "From this day forward, I'm forsaking all others to be with you and only you." That's the commitment to each other—and to God—that Tammy and I made that day in the middle of May all those years ago.

Our wedding was similar to many couples' weddings, I'm guessing. We invited a couple hundred people to join us at our home church to witness our vows and celebrate our union. We played music, including the traditional processional when Tammy came down the aisle looking so beautiful in her white wedding gown. Our pastor talked about the significance of marriage according to God's Word and then led us through our vows to the moment of placing rings on each other's fingers.

Tammy and I still wear those wedding bands today, and they mean the same thing now that they did then. They provide an outward expression of the inward devotion we maintain to one another. They signal to everyone around us that we're taken, committed to each other, bound by our vows of marriage.

Similarly, when we commit to following Jesus, we take on a symbol to demonstrate our devotion.

In fact, you might say it's a slam dunk.

WHY GET BAPTIZED?

It's important that any covenant is sealed in the presence of witnesses, and salvation is no different. Baptism serves as the wedding band of the Christian faith, an outward symbol of the internal commitment we've made to God. When anyone asks me why they should get baptized, I usually give them three reasons, all based on what we see in the Bible. First and foremost, we follow the example set by Jesus himself. Before he began his public ministry, Jesus went to Galilee to the Jordan River to be baptized by his cousin John. We're told, "As soon as Jesus was baptized, he went up out of the water. At that moment heaven was opened, and he saw the Spirit of God descending like a dove and alighting on him. And a voice from heaven said, 'This is my Son, whom I love; with him I am well pleased'" (Matthew 3:16–17).

Think about it. If God's own Son was baptized to show his commitment to his Father and his Father's mission on earth, then shouldn't that be reason enough for us to follow suit? It certainly was for the more than two dozen people mentioned in the New Testament who were baptized after committing to follow Christ. I like what Paul wrote in his letter to the Corinthians: "Follow my example, as I follow the example of Christ" (1 Corinthians 11:1).

We're not merely given a suggestion to be baptized if we feel like it. Jesus told his disciples, "Whoever believes and is baptized will be saved, but whoever does not believe will be condemned" (Mark 16:16). Believers who are serious about their faith, whether they're introverts or extroverts, shy or bold, quiet or loud, should view baptism as an act of obedience.

Another reason to get baptized is to demonstrate the change that has occurred in our lives. "In baptism we show that we have been saved from death and doom by the resurrection of Christ; not because our bodies are washed clean by the water but because in being baptized we are turning to God and asking him to cleanse our *hearts* from sin" (1 Peter 3:21 TLB). If our hearts really have been transformed, then our actions will reveal that change over time. But there's no better way to announce that change immediately than to let others see us take this symbolic action.

While visiting the Jordan River in Israel, I was fascinated to learn how baptisms have traditionally been performed. Individuals dress in all white and then place old, dirty, tattered clothes over them. As they go under the surface of the river, they remove their old clothes and emerge exuberantly in white, letting the worn-out garments be carried away downstream. That makes the symbolism that much clearer—before Christ we're sinful; after we have Christ, we're washed clean.

Finally, baptism is a public declaration of the personal commitment we've made. It's the natural, logical outcome of our decision to trust Jesus. You might be tempted to think that baptism is optional or preferential. People tell me, "My faith is private, so I don't need to do the baptism thing." But when I ask them to point out this teaching in the Bible, no one has ever been able to show me any evidence. There isn't any! Your faith is not a secret. You don't have to preach on a park bench, but you should be willing to let others see the choice you have made and its impact on the rest of your life.

One of my favorite Christian songs, "I Have Decided to Follow Jesus," makes this bold declaration of faith its anthem. Not long ago, I learned the story behind this song, and it stopped me in my tracks. Apparently, the song was written after the death of a newly converted Christian in India. This man and his immediate family had renounced Hinduism, along with the more primitive beliefs of their local tribe. When the tribal chief found out, he had this family brought before him and ordered them to renounce their faith in Christ or face execution. The man replied, "I have decided to follow Jesus—no turning back." The angry chief then killed the man's children, but still the man would not deny his Christian faith. As his wife was executed, the man insisted, "Though no one joins me, still I will follow." Finally, as he himself was being put to death, the man proclaimed, "The cross before me, the world behind me." The chief, and later the entire village, became believers because of the dramatic testimony of this martyr of the faith.[1]

Most of us will not face such persecution for following Jesus, and yet we're reluctant to let others know about our faith through the act of baptism. But we must remember what Jesus said: "Whoever acknowledges me before others, I will also acknowledge before my Father in heaven. But whoever disowns me before others, I will disown before my Father in heaven" (Matthew 10:32–33). Why would we not want to share our most meaningful relationship with everyone around us, just as we would an engagement, a marriage, or the birth of a child? Certainly in Scripture those who made this important commitment wanted others to know what they had done. We're told, "Those who accepted [Peter's] message were baptized" (Acts 2:41). And Acts 8:12 says, "When they believed Philip as he proclaimed the good news of the kingdom of God and the name of Jesus Christ, they were baptized, both men and women." We also see the example of Simon the sorcerer, who "himself believed and was baptized" (v. 13).

Ultimately, baptism illustrates the internal commitment we've made. Just as my wedding ring represents my wedding vows to Tammy, baptism indicates to others our dedication to following, serving, and obeying Christ. It's that simple.

YOUR NEXT STEP ON THE JOURNEY

Each of us has a unique spiritual journey and relationship with God, but topics like baptism—which are embedded within the four steps of knowing God, finding freedom, discovering purpose, and making a difference—are relevant to all of us. We just need to understand how each step relates to the others.

Some of these steps are sequential—for instance, your first big step is always going to be accepting Jesus into your life. Next, it makes sense to obey his command to be baptized as an outward symbol of your inward commitment. Because all our lives are different, though, and because God has his own unique timing, many of these spiritual steps will not follow a linear route as much as show up along the way as you hike through uncharted territory. So, don't worry if you waited years after accepting Christ before being baptized.

As you seek the answer to "What's next?" in this part of your journey, I encourage you to spend some time in prayer, assessing where you are in your relationship with God. What needs to happen for you to align your commitment to him with the way you live your life each day? Ask the Holy Spirit to guide you and give you insight into your next step. Trust that he will show you the way and reveal God's path as you walk in faith. If you have not been baptized after inviting Jesus into your heart, make an appointment with your pastor or other church leader to discuss when you can be baptized. If you have already been baptized, think back on your experience. What did it mean to you at that time? What does it mean to you now?

CHAPTER TWO

PRAYER

CONVERSATIONS WITH GOD

I'm probably not supposed to admit this since I'm a pastor, but prayer isn't easy for me. I've never felt that praying is something I do particularly well. I've always envied pastors who pray so eloquently or those who talk about the hours they spend with God every day, causing me to wonder, *What am I doing wrong?*

I suspect I'm not alone in feeling this way. Most people seem to have an idea about what prayer should be and feel like they fall short. But what if our ideas about prayer are not what God wants? What if there's not a "right way" to pray any more than there's a right way to enjoy talking to someone you love, like your spouse, kids, or closest friends? What if God just wants to spend time with us, hear our hearts, and have a simple and meaningful conversation?

WHAT IT TAKES TO PRAY

If you grew up in church as I did, you were probably aware of prayer from an early age: hearing others called on to pray spontaneously, being taught about prayer from the Bible, or memorizing the Lord's Prayer. The practice itself can be intimidating, especially when we're asked to pray aloud in a group. We end up worried about what we're going to say, wanting it to sound sincere as well as appropriate for the setting. We get distracted by the person squeezing our hand too tight or the cold, barely there palm of the person on the other side.

I'll never forget the first time I attended an all-night prayer meeting. Yes, that's right—all night! At certain intervals, everyone would gather to pray together, but most of the time we were supposed to pray on our own. I went to a prayer room, got down on my knees, and started praying. I quickly went through my usual items and began widening my prayer net to include people I didn't always think to pray for.

I mentioned every distant cousin I could remember. From extended family and close friends and acquaintances, I moved on to people I didn't know—movie stars, the LSU football team, and the president. Then I went global, praying for every country that came to mind, its leaders, missionaries there, and all the people living there who needed to know the Lord. After praying for so many people and places for so long, I felt a sense of accomplishment and figured at least an hour or two had likely passed since I began.

Looking at my watch, though, I saw that barely fifteen minutes had gone by.

I knew then it was going to be a long night.

That experience left me feeling like I simply wasn't spiritual enough to be a prayer warrior. I was sure my mind shouldn't have been jumping around from topic to topic or drifting away to matters entirely unrelated to my prayer requests. You know, things like, *Boy, my knees are killing me. And I'm so hungry—I wonder when we're going to eat. Sure could go for some pizza right now. Which reminds me, I need to stop at the store and get some cereal and milk. And the oil needs to be changed in the car—I've been meaning to do that for weeks . . .*

I assumed I must not have what it takes. Surely a real prayer warrior wouldn't be so unfocused.

Later, though, I found a passage from Chuck Swindoll that expressed exactly how I felt about my prayer inadequacies:

> To be painfully honest with you, most of the stuff I have ever read or heard said about prayer has either left me under a ton-and-a-half truckload of guilt or wearied me with pious-sounding clichés and meaningless god-talk. Because I didn't spend two or three grueling hours a day on my knees as dear Dr. So-and-So did . . .

or because I wasn't able to weave dozens of Scripture verses through my prayer . . . or because I had not been successful in moving mountains, I picked up the distinct impression that I was out to lunch when it came to this part of the Christian life.[1]

Have you ever felt this way? Do you secretly dread having to pray aloud in a group because you're afraid others will realize the truth about you and prayer? Despite whatever you may or may not have learned about prayer, do you still feel as though there's a right way to do it and you're simply not able to master it?

Regardless of the impressions or ideals you associate with prayer, regardless of your feelings about your own prayer life, put all that aside for the rest of this chapter. Let's rethink every idea you've ever had about prayer and what's required when you pray.

Over the years, I've realized that we are often the main problem when it comes to our prayer lives. The assumptions and expectations we attach to the practice of prayer prevent us from conversing naturally and unself-consciously with God. Prayer is not about reciting Christian phrases or using fancy religious words. It's not about sounding like your pastor or whomever you admire for the way they pray. It's not even about sitting in a circle and holding hands with others.

What does it take to pray? A heart willing to talk to God, to listen to him, and to hear his voice. Prayer

24

is about his Spirit and our spirit connecting with each other. It's about real fellowship, open and honest heart-to-heart talks with one another. It's about intimate conversation.

PRAY WITHOUT CEASING

How can we shift the way we think about prayer into something more natural and enjoyable? How can we let go of feeling like we're on the witness stand or giving a speech and instead view prayer as an easy, relaxed bond shared with someone we love?

Here's the secret: Don't make prayer an event or an obligation. Let it simply be an ongoing conversation with God each day. Paul reinforces this idea when he tells us, "Pray continually" (1 Thessalonians 5:17). It's not a stop-start activity like physical exercise to be practiced and performed. Instead, it's ongoing, fluid, dynamic communication back and forth between a loving Father and his children.

God's Word tells us, "Remain in me, as I also remain in you. No branch can bear fruit by itself; it must remain in the vine. Neither can you bear fruit unless you remain in me. I am the vine; you are the branches. If you remain in me and I in you, you will bear much fruit; apart from me you can do nothing" (John 15:4–5). Notice the organic, intimate union this passage illustrates between us and God. We are like branches attached to a vine. The vine nourishes and sustains the growth of the branches, giving them life. And the way we stay continuously connected to this source of life is through prayer.

Prayer was intended to be an ongoing conversation, like a text thread with a friend that goes on all day. The great British evangelist, Smith Wigglesworth (what a great name!) once instructed, "Never pray more than twenty minutes, but never go more than twenty minutes without praying."[2]

We can be intentional about talking to God every day, the same way we schedule other priorities or find time for the people we love. Even when it's not convenient or comfortable, we honor our commitments to our loved ones and take their calls or respond to their texts. If I'm away from home and speaking at a conference, I make sure I find time to check in with my wife, Tammy. She doesn't have to remind me or force me to do it. My heart misses her, so I don't even have to think about wanting to hear her voice and connect about our day.

Make prayer a priority until it's a natural part of your day.

TAKE TIME TO PRAY

Just as marriage requires effort and commitment, our relationship with God requires us to follow through on making him our number-one priority. That means we have to find time to pray. If I tell my wife I love her but never have time to talk to her, she will begin to question the depth of my love and commitment. Similarly, we have to do more than just say we want to know God. We have to make time to talk with him and continue the conversation from day to day.

This deliberate, ongoing dialogue with God is exemplified by one of my favorite prayer warriors from the Bible, the prophet Daniel. Scripture tells us, "Now when Daniel learned that the decree had been published, he went home to his upstairs room where the windows opened toward Jerusalem. Three times a day he got down on his knees and prayed, giving thanks to his God, just as he had done before" (Daniel 6:10).

Even after he had been taken captive by the Babylonians, along with the entire nation of Israel, Daniel kept his prayer life the same. It can be so tempting, when something unexpected disrupts your schedule, to cut the most important appointment: your time with God. Daniel's example reminds us that no matter what, we should make prayer a priority.

I can't compare to Daniel, but I do have an office in the basement of our house where I love to pray most days. I go there early in the morning before anyone else wakes up, light a candle, and read my Bible. Then I sit in my soft chair and just talk to God.

FIND A PLACE TO PRAY

You may already have your own special place to pray, but if you don't, I encourage you to find a specific spot. It doesn't have to be like my basement office or a place like anyone else's. Your prayer location can be as simple as your favorite chair by the window or the supply cupboard at work. The key is having a place where you know you likely won't be interrupted or distracted, where you can relax, still your soul, and talk to God. For most of us, this means turning off our phones and leaving tablets and laptops in another room.

We see that even Jesus had a special place where he regularly talked to his Father: "Very early in the morning, while it was still dark, Jesus got up, left the house and went off to a solitary place, where he prayed" (Mark 1:35). In our hectic, electronically connected world, finding our own solitary place isn't easy, but if Jesus' example is any indication, it's clearly important.

Your prayer place doesn't have to be stationary. Sometimes I like to walk through my neighborhood and pray. Or I pray in the car on the way to an appointment or to my office. I put on some worship music and feel like I can say anything on my heart just as loudly as I want. It's similar to the freedom you feel when you hear a favorite song on the radio and sing along. Only you're talking to God.

HAVE A PLAN FOR PRAYER

While it's great to share what's on your heart when you pray, it's also helpful to use some kind of structure. And don't take it from me—take it from Jesus, who taught his disciples to pray based on what we now refer to as the Lord's Prayer. This model was not intended to be a prayer we memorize to recite verbatim, although that's certainly okay. It was more of a guide, since Jesus knew that the Jewish rabbis taught in outline form and that's what his followers would be used to.

Being good Hebrew students, Jesus' disciples would have learned how to pray the ancient Jewish prayers. But they must have noticed something different, something so personal and powerful, about the way Jesus prayed, because they asked their Master about this distinction: "One day Jesus was praying in a certain place. When he finished, one of his disciples said to him, 'Lord, teach us to pray'" (Luke 11:1).

In response, Jesus said, "This is how you should pray" (v. 2 NLT), meaning simply that they should say something like what he was about to model for them. Then he prayed:

"Our Father in heaven, hallowed be your name, your kingdom come, your will be done, on earth as it is in heaven. Give us today our daily bread. And forgive us our debts, as we also have forgiven our debtors. And lead us not into temptation, but deliver us from the evil one, for yours is the kingdom and the power and the glory forever." (Matthew 6:9–13)

Let's look at each of the seven key phrases in Jesus' model and see what we can learn about his plan for prayer:

"OUR FATHER IN HEAVEN"

First, we are to connect with God relationally. He is our heavenly Father, not some distant, detached deity we can never know. The Bible tells us, "You have not received a spirit that makes you fearful slaves. Instead, you received God's Spirit when he adopted you as his own children. Now we call him, 'Abba, Father'" (Romans 8:15 NLT). The almighty God, Creator of the universe, loves for us to call him our Daddy! So, when you pray, remind yourself of your intimate bond with God by addressing him as your loving Father.

"HALLOWED BE YOUR NAME"

Next, we are to worship his name. Why should we worship him? Because worship gets our focus off ourselves and onto God. It shifts our attention to him instead of our own lives, circumstances, and requests. In worship, we attune our hearts to an attitude of awe and gratitude.

One way to worship is to meditate on the names of

God. Did you know that God has many names? In the Old Testament we find at least eight different names of God formed from Hebrew compound words. In the Bible, a name usually refers to some aspect of a person's character. No surprise then that these names of God reveal or emphasize different aspects of his character. For example, "GOD's name is a place of protection—good people can run there and be safe" (Proverbs 18:10 THE MESSAGE).

Here's a brief list of some of the other names of God:

Righteousness: He makes me clean.
Sanctifier: He has called me and set me apart.
Healer: He heals all my diseases.
Banner of Victory: He has defeated my enemy.
Shepherd: He speaks to me and leads me.
Peace: He is my peace in every storm.
Provider: He supplies all my needs.
There: He is ever-present to comfort and help me.

Knowing and using these various names for God allows us to appreciate the different facets of his character and puts our hearts in right alignment with him.

"YOUR KINGDOM COME, YOUR WILL BE DONE, ON EARTH AS IT IS IN HEAVEN"

We are to pray according to God's agenda first. Doing so helps us keep the right perspective and acknowledge our own limitations. We're the creation; he is the

Creator. His plans are always going to be higher, better, and holier than ours, and we demonstrate our trust in him when we surrender our own plans to his. Scripture assures us, "He will always give you all you need from day to day if you will make the Kingdom of God your primary concern" (Luke 12:31 TLB).

What are God's primary concerns? First, he loves all his children, so he remains in constant pursuit of those who are lost and separated from him. He also wants us to honor and obey those in authority; he sets up positions of authority to bring about his will in our lives. So, we pray for those who are lost and for our parents, teachers, pastors, bosses, and leaders in government at every level.

Finally, we pray for God's will to be done in our own lives. We ask God to direct our steps, and we trust him with each of those steps we take. Again, we let go of what we so often try to control, force, or manipulate to happen so we can receive direction and guidance from the One who knows best.

"GIVE US THIS DAY OUR DAILY BREAD"

When the Bible mentions "our daily bread," it's not just referring to what we eat each day; it's a call to depend on our Father for everything. Bread represents the necessities of life—all our physical and material needs. God wants us to pray instead of worry. When we pray for things we need, we don't have to worry about them, because God has promised to provide all our needs (Philippians 4:19).

Also, notice that Jesus said to pray for our "daily" bread—not weekly, monthly, or annual. I was scrolling through the calendar on my phone recently and was amazed to see it ran through every month until beyond 2100! Talk about planning in advance! We may be tempted to worry about what has already happened in the past or what might happen in the future. God wants us to focus on today, the present, and what we need for now.

Our needs vary, of course. What do you need today? Energy to make it through the day? More money to pay unexpected bills? Wisdom to talk to your teenager about a conflict? Patience to deal with your coworkers? Remember how God provided manna for the people of Israel after he delivered them from captivity in Egypt? God gave the manna, but it spoiled if the people tried to keep it longer than a day. God wanted his people to trust him moment by moment.

The same is true when it comes to what God wants from us. Scripture instructs us, "Do not be anxious about anything, but in every situation, by prayer and peti-tion, with thanksgiving, present your requests to God" (Philippians 4:6). Basically, we have two choices: panic or pray. And this verse instructs us to pray in *every* situa-tion. We can pray about anything and everything.

I would be embarrassed to tell you some of the prayer

requests I've made in my life. Some seem silly or petty or of minor importance. But my prayer requests don't embarrass God. Anything worth worrying about is worth praying about. After all, as the psalmist wrote, "I look up to the mountains—does my help come from there? My help comes from the LORD, who made heaven and earth!" (Psalm 121:1–2 NLT). If we prayed as much as we worried, we'd have a lot less to worry about. Give God your worries. Ask God for what you want and need, and then trust him for the answer.

"FORGIVE US OUR DEBTS, AS WE ALSO HAVE FORGIVEN OUR DEBTORS"

Jesus instructs us to make sure our hearts are right with God and right with other people. All of us have regrets. All of us make mistakes. All of us fall short. Despite our best efforts, it happens again and again and again. The Bible says, "If we confess our sins, he is faithful and just and will forgive us our sins and purify us from all unrighteousness" (1 John 1:9).

God promises, "I will cleanse you," and he forgives us instantly, totally, freely, repeatedly, continuously. One of the benefits of prayer is that we can unload our guilt. There is no reason for Christians to carry guilt in their lives day after day. *None at all.* If you are, you're not taking advantage of what Jesus Christ did on the cross. Give God your guilt.

God wants to forgive you. He says so over and over

throughout his Word. Ask him to check your heart, to search your motives and thoughts, and to bring to light any areas that stand between you and him or between you and other people. Then, just as God gives us grace, we are to forgive anyone who has hurt or offended us in any way. We can even forgive them in advance!

Without a doubt, in life we will be hurt. Sometimes intentionally. Sometimes unintentionally. How we handle those hurts determines our happiness. For our own happiness, we must learn to forgive and to practice forgiveness on a regular basis. This is the only part of the Lord's Prayer that Jesus gave further commentary on after he taught the prayer: "For if you forgive other people when they sin against you, your heavenly Father will also forgive you. But if you do not forgive others their sins, your Father will not forgive your sins" (Matthew 6:14–15).

It's not that God is unwilling to forgive us before we forgive those who sin against us; it's that we're blocking our own path when we sit in unforgiveness. Someone once came to John Wesley and said, "I just can't forgive that person! They hurt me too badly." Wesley thought for a moment and said, "Then I hope you never sin!"[3]

The Bible says to forgive and be forgiven. The two commands are interrelated. For your own sake, let go of the past. If somebody hurt you, let go of it. Release them—*and* release yourself. That's one of the many benefits of prayer. It helps you unload.

Prayer is nothing if not practical!

"AND LEAD US NOT INTO TEMPTATION, BUT DELIVER US FROM THE EVIL ONE"

Here Jesus reminds us not only that evil is a reality in the world we live in, but also that we must engage in spiritual warfare. God's Word says, "For our struggle is not against flesh and blood, but against the rulers, against the authorities, against the powers of this dark world and against the spiritual forces of evil in the heavenly realms" (Ephesians 6:12).

Take your stand against the enemy and fight the good fight of faith. Every lie that the enemy has told you should be replaced with the truth of God's Word. Prayer is not only communion with God; it's confrontation with the enemy.

God has given us authority over the devil, but it's our job to exercise that authority. How do we exercise this power? There's no one right way, but here's how I often do it. I imagine everything the enemy wants me to do—succumb to temptations, indulge bad attitudes, lash out at others—and I say out loud, "No, not today! Not going to happen." And then I go through the armor of God (vv. 10–18)—piece by piece—and I put it on. Then I think about all the places where I feel under attack, and I ask God to help me, to cover and protect me. It works!

Where are you being attacked? How is the enemy coming after you right now? What's out of control in your life? Give it to God. That's raw prayer material. Pray something like, "God, this is out of control in my life. I can't control my temper. God, I can't control my wandering thoughts. I can't control my appetite. I can't control this dependency. I can't control my tendency to . . ." Whatever it is, give it to God and ask him to intervene.

Another area where Satan sometimes attacks us involves our fears. What are you afraid of? Be honest and simply say, "God, I'm scared to death about the future . . . or this new job . . . or that I'm out of work . . . or that I've got a problem . . . or that I'll never get married." No matter what it is, give it to God and allow him to overcome that fear in your heart with his truth! Then cry out, "I sought the LORD, and he answered me; he delivered me from all fears" (Psalm 34:4).

Prayer allows you to fight the good fight.

"FOR YOURS IS THE KINGDOM AND THE POWER AND THE GLORY FOREVER"

Finally, express faith in God's ability. Scripture tells us, "Ah, Sovereign LORD, you have made the heavens and the earth by your great power and outstretched arm. Nothing is too hard for you" (Jeremiah 32:17). End your prayer time by reminding yourself of God's ability. Return to praise, and make your faith declarations. End in the victory that Jesus has already secured:

"Yours is the kingdom"—all rule belongs to you!
"Yours is the power"—all mightiness flows
    from you!
"Yours is the glory"—your victory is complete!

Even when you don't feel victorious, remind yourself of the truth of God's Word. Don't let your emotions dictate how and when and why you pray. Talk to God. Open your heart. Listen to him. Praise him and give him thanks for all the blessings in your life. Praise him for who he is and how you are able to talk to him directly.

YOUR NEXT STEP ON THE JOURNEY

We sometimes make prayer harder than it has to be when really it is just talking with God. And the more you do it, the more comfortable and natural it feels. You don't have to use fancy words or English from the King James Version of the Bible. God isn't grading you on how well you communicate—in fact, there's nothing you can do to impress him. He simply wants to know your heart, to listen to you, to talk with you.

So, start today. Ask someone you know and trust to be a prayer partner with you, and then set a weekly time to get together, share prayer requests, and pray. Commit to praying for each other the rest of the week as well.

I also encourage you to attend a prayer meeting at your church. Even if you don't pray out loud in the group, you can enjoy praying with others and becoming more relaxed with prayer by seeing the various ways others pray. You may eventually want to join a prayer team, a group dedicated to lifting up the needs of the church along with specific personal requests.

The key to prayer is to just do it! Pray continually. Keep an ongoing conversation with God each day. You'll be amazed at how prayer makes you, and your relationship with God, stronger.

CHAPTER THREE

THE BIBLE

LETTING GOD'S WORD
SPEAK TO YOU

Most days start with me waking up and heading to my office in our basement at home. I'm still in my sweatpants and some old ugly T-shirt Tammy wishes I'd let her throw away. In my office I light a candle, though not necessarily for any spiritual reasons; I just like the fresh scent and the ambience it creates. I'm not awake enough to pray just yet, so I pick up my Bible, one I was given shortly after I gave my life to Jesus, and I turn to the place marked from the day before.

I know my way around its pages by now and use underlined words and my handwritten notes in the margins as points of navigation. I don't have a stack of study Bibles and a set of concordances and theological encyclopedias on floor-to-ceiling shelves beside me. I don't keep three pairs of glasses handy, like C. S. Lewis did, to adjust my vision to different font sizes in various texts (thank goodness for bifocals!). It's just me and the Word.

Maybe I'm a Bible geek, but I'm still genuinely excited to read God's Word each morning, to reflect on it, meditate on it, and carry it with me into my day. In fact, my favorite day of the week is what I call my study day, when I immerse myself in studying the Bible, researching whatever I need to know to inform and enhance my understanding. I love delivering the message God gives me each week, but there's something about being alone with his Word that thrills me.

You can have this same excitement too. You don't have to be a pastor. Or go to Bible college. Or know ancient Hebrew and Greek.

Many people tell me they don't read the Bible because they're overwhelmed by it. They don't know where to start. They don't really understand what they're reading or how it fits into their understanding of God and his plan for us. They struggle to see its relevancy and how it applies to their lives today. But it doesn't have to be this way. In fact, the Bible is the most relevant wisdom there is, and it includes a wealth of instruction just waiting to be mined.

Let's fall in love with God's Word together.

Let's allow God to speak to us through it.

But since it's tough to love something we don't really understand, let's start by thinking about what we need to know.

THE GOOD BOOK

The word *bible* simply means "book." It comes from the Greek *biblios*, which originated in the Greek city of Byblos, the largest importer of papyrus in the ancient world and, therefore, a major center for producing books. While lots of bibles—I'm using this word generically here—were printed, distributed, and read over the course of history, the Bible, referring to God's Word, stands above and beyond them.

Simply put, the Bible is not a normal book. It's the *Hagios Biblios*, the Holy Bible (since *hagios* in Greek means "sacred" or "set apart"). There is no other book like it, and there never will be. The Bible is the most read book in history, the bestselling book of all time, and the most-translated book, now available in most of the human languages and dialects known today. It was written in three different languages over a period of sixteen hundred years in more than a dozen countries on three continents by people from all walks of life. Although most of them did not know each other or even live in the same time period, they all got part of the same story.

Many other belief systems have a primary holy book written by one person. The Quran was written by Muhammad. The Analects of Confucius is believed to have been written by one and the same, much like the writings of Buddha. When a book has one writer, it makes sense to expect a kind of consistent, uniform style and voice to the book. The Bible, however, was written by a unique group of poets, prophets, farmers, kings, soldiers, shepherds, princes, priests, historians, fishermen, tax collectors, scholars, businessmen, and doctors. It was written in caves, ships, palaces, prisons, and deserts. It includes incredibly personal and vulnerable cries from the heart, such as those found in the Psalms, as well as history and personal letters.

Despite all these unique differences, despite having almost forty writers, the Bible still has only one author—God himself. We're told, "All Scripture is God-breathed and is useful for teaching, rebuking, correcting and training in righteousness, so that the servant of God may be thoroughly equipped for every good work" (2 Timothy 3:16–17). In many ways, the Bible is God's autobiography. It's inspired with his breath and infused with his power. The living Word gives us his plan of redemption for all people.

And the Bible speaks to us as individuals, providing a foundation for our lives.

BUILDING YOUR LIFE ON GOD'S WORD

If you want to know God, if you want to take the next step in your journey of faith, then no matter where you are, you can build your life on God's Word. It is the bedrock foundation of who we are and all we do, not an optional part of our faith that we can choose to ignore if we don't like it or understand it. We read in Matthew:

> "These words I speak to you are not incidental additions to your life, homeowner improvements to your standard of living. They are foundational words, words to build a life on. If you work these words into your life, you are like a smart carpenter who built his house on solid rock." (7:24 THE MESSAGE)

If building our lives on God's Word is not optional, then it becomes a practical matter of how. The Christian life is nothing if not practical, and the Bible provides us with a kind of owner's manual from our Creator. God knows what's true and what's best for us, so we can trust him to reveal instruction for every aspect of our lives. But how do you relate to Scripture and incorporate it as the foundation for your life? Let's take a look at several guidelines I've found helpful through the years.

1. WELCOME THE BIBLE INTO YOUR LIFE AND ACCEPT ITS AUTHORITY.

You can't have a take-it-or-leave-it attitude toward God's Word. You can't pretend it's outdated and doesn't apply to us anymore. The way you perceive the Bible makes a huge difference in your attitude and in your full acceptance of God's authority over your life. As Paul wrote to the church in Thessalonica, "We also thank God continually because, when you received the word of God, which you heard from us, you accepted it not as a human word, but as it actually is, the word of God, which is indeed at work in you who believe" (1 Thessalonians 2:13).

When you're in a relationship with God through his Holy Spirit dwelling in you, you're also in a relationship with his Word. Receiving and accepting the Bible as the actual Word of God, acknowledging that its pages are divinely inspired and recorded, requires you to ascribe an authority to it that no other source has.

This is significant, because it elevates God's Word above any other source of teaching in your life: what you learned (or didn't learn) from your parents, your education in school, all that other people have told you, other books regardless of the author, and what you read online. In other words, no other books, verses, or ideas may ever be placed beside the Bible as equal in authority or revelation.

All preaching, teaching, and prophesying, along with any other communication being declared in the name of the Lord, are to be subject to measurement by the content of God's Word. This eliminates most of the gray areas of life, a fact we may not always appreciate. If you're like me, you may be tempted to think you're the exception and God will allow you loopholes he doesn't allow for others. For example, you agree that telling a lie is a sin but justify leaving out the full truth when your spouse asks you a question because you don't want to hurt their feelings.

But God's Word does not make exceptions—God's authority applies to all of us. To grow in your faith, you must settle the issue of authority in your life. Once this matter is settled, you might be surprised how liberated you feel. God's guidelines provide healthy, holy boundaries for your life. Wisdom for everything you face, from marriage to parenting to personal grief to community celebration, can be found in Scripture. The Bible helps you live your life with more peace, more joy, and more fulfillment.

But you have to let God's Word be the final word.

2. INCLUDE THE BIBLE IN YOUR LIFE ON A REGULAR BASIS.

Including God's Word in your life means regularly spending time reading it, studying it, thinking about it and meditating on it, praying it, and using it. Whether it's in the morning, on your lunch break, before you go to bed—whenever you can best focus your mind and heart on engaging with it—make Bible reading a daily priority. If you go days or weeks without talking to a spouse or loved one, you drift apart and become disconnected. The same is true for our relationship with God if we're not in the Word.

I'm passionate about daily Bible reading. It, along with prayer, establishes our regular communication with God. Our bodies require daily nourishment, and so do our souls. When we spend time in the Word, we're feeding ourselves with the Bread of Life and enjoying a spiritual meal with God. Sometimes I like to skip meals and fast, using the time I would have been eating to receive spiritual sustenance from Scripture instead. Jesus himself said, "It is written: 'Man shall not live on bread alone, but on every word that comes from the mouth of God'" (Matthew 4:4).

In addition to reading the Bible in our personal time, we are also to listen to God's Word. We're told, "So then faith comes by hearing, and hearing by the word of God" (Romans 10:17 NKJV). By listening to God's Word—from preachers, teachers, church leaders, and other followers of Jesus—we grow in our understanding and appreciation of everything God packs into the Bible. But I'd caution us all against growing too comfortable with only hearing the Word and not reading it ourselves.

Sometimes people tell me they don't need to read their Bibles because they're in church so often that they hear it all the time. While I'm thrilled that they're being nourished by the Word when they're in church, there is still no substitute for the direct, personal encounter you have with God in his Word. So no matter how much you're hearing from others, own and cherish your time in the Bible.

3. MAKE A DELIBERATE PLAN FOR PRIORITIZING YOUR TIME IN GOD'S WORD.

The plan for your time reading and studying the Bible can be as unique as you are. Remember when you were in school how some students liked to underline everything and use highlighters in the text, while others took notes in a separate notebook? Or how some people liked listening to music as they studied, while others needed absolute quiet? We're all different and learn in different ways. Use what you know about yourself and how you learn best, and apply it to your plan for reading Scripture.

For example, I like the digital modes of the Bible and use them when it's convenient or when I'm on the go, but I still carry my old dog-eared Holy Bible with me. There's just something about being able to turn the pages and hold my finger in one place while flipping to look at another. I know there are comparable ways to do this digitally, but for me it's not the same. My old Bible feels so personal with many years' worth of notes, underlining, questions, and references in its margins.

Being consistent about when you read your Bible is important too. Set aside time when you know you won't be rushed and you'll be able to focus without interruption.

Turn off your phone (another reason not to read a digital version—you might be tempted to respond to texts, emails, or calls). Make it an enjoyable routine, something you look forward to doing instead of feeling obligated to do it so you can check it off your list.

The key is to make reading God's Word a priority, not an afterthought or something we squeeze in if we remember it. Like physical exercise, we benefit most with a routine that fits into our lifestyle. Think through your current season of life, review your present schedule, and establish a consistent time to learn from and listen to God through his Word.

4. CHOOSE A STRATEGY FOR HOW YOU WILL READ THE BIBLE.

I'm not going to tell you not to simply flip through the Bible and randomly read wherever you land in the pages. But, as with most things, I think it makes more sense and will help your understanding if you have a reading plan. Choosing a strategy for how you will read helps you break down the full Bible into smaller, more accessible parts, which, in turn, makes it feel less overwhelming.

For this reason, I like the One Year Bible. With sixty-six books—that's thirty-nine in the Old Testament and twenty-seven in the New—and a total of one thousand one hundred eighty-nine chapters, the Bible might seem like Mount Everest. But if you break down your reading to three or four chapters a day, as recommended in the One Year Bible, you can easily pace yourself and read through the entirety of God's Word in the next year.

If that still feels too daunting, consider other possible ways to approach your reading strategy. For instance, you might focus on the Gospels—Matthew, Mark, Luke, and John. If you read three chapters a day, you will complete all eighty-nine chapters in a month. Of course, you can also slow your pace and read one chapter a day for three months.

Another approach is to focus on the Psalms. Psalms has a total of one hundred fifty chapters, so you can decide how many chapters you read each day and how long it will take you to finish reading them all. Similarly, you can take the thirty-one chapters of Proverbs and focus on one each day for a month.

You could choose any of these approaches or even another not mentioned here, but it's worth considering ahead of time what will be most helpful so you don't get overwhelmed looking at the sixty-six books of the Bible and then stop before you start.

5. DON'T JUST READ THE BIBLE; LET THE BIBLE READ YOU.

Invite God to speak to you as you read his Word. Be attentive; listen to what the Holy Spirit may reveal to you about yourself and your life. Don't just read the words by scanning your eyes across the lines on the page; slow down and absorb them. Read them over and over again until you've allowed God to speak to you about what he sees in you and how he's calling you to follow him more fully. Personalize what you're reading; realize it's not only historical or poetic, but inspired and timeless as well. God's Word is the same yesterday, today, and tomorrow.

When you study and meditate on God's Word, you increase your understanding of it and its application to your life. As the psalmist wrote, "I have hidden your word in my heart that I might not sin against you" (Psalm 119:11). So much richness is available as you study the Bible. If you feel stuck reading on your own, remember that with so much information at your fingertips via your phone, laptop, or tablet, you can research virtually all parts of the passage you're reading. You can also take advantage of being part of a small group, learning from and discussing with others what they understand from the passage of Scripture you're reading together. Or your group could participate in one of the many excellent thematic studies available—on finances, parenting, relationships, and so on—with curriculum to guide you as you study the Bible in these areas. These group studies usually require you to spend some time in the Word between sessions, helping you to be deliberate and strategic individually as well as collectively.

6. LOOK FOR WAYS TO APPLY THE BIBLE IN YOUR EVERYDAY LIFE.

God's Word is clear: "Do not merely listen to the word, and so deceive yourselves. Do what it says" (James 1:22). Again, the Bible remains so practically relevant for our lives today. Jesus said, "Everyone who hears these words of mine and puts them into practice is like a wise man who built his house on the rock" (Matthew 7:24). His instruction, just like the example of his life, provides clear resources and remedies for anything and everything we face.

Although I believed this truth before, it really hit home shortly after Tammy and I were married and our apartment was robbed. We were distraught over losing our stuff, but also felt angry and violated that someone had broken into our home. We began to pray together about it and to look in God's Word for relevant passages. We compiled a list of verses about how to handle our feelings of anger, fear, violation, and loss.

Ever since that incident, anytime I have a problem, big or small, I find a verse that applies and focus on it and not on the problem or my inability to solve it. God is bigger than any situation you will encounter, no matter how devastating or infuriating or painful it may seem in the moment. Instead of focusing inward and brooding on circumstances or the ways others have offended you, channel your energy and attention into the timeless truth of God's Word.

Whatever you're going through, find a verse for the situation and meditate on it. Here are a few of my favorites to get you started:

- **Battles**—1 John 4:4; Luke 10:19; Romans 8:37
  ("We are more than conquerors.")

- **Money**—Psalm 1:1–3; Philippians 4:19 ("My God will meet all your needs.")
- **Fear**—Psalm 27:1 ("The LORD is my light and my salvation—whom shall I fear?")
- **Sickness**—Psalm 103:2–3 ("Praise the Lord . . . [who] heals all your diseases.")
- **Confidence**—2 Corinthians 3:6 ("He has made us competent.")
- **Safety**—Psalm 121:8 ("The LORD will watch over your coming and going.")
- **Dentist**—Psalm 81:10 ("Open wide your mouth and I will fill it.")

YOUR NEXT STEP ON THE JOURNEY

Making the Bible the foundation of your life is not hard. Some people feel resistant because they don't have a theology degree or don't believe they're smart enough to understand it. Others view the Bible as simply too difficult to tackle, too overwhelming. Some may mismanage their time, surfing social media or binge-watching Netflix, instead of making their time in the Word the priority they want it to be.

If you remember that reading the Bible is about *relationship*—not theology, homework, or literary analysis—then it becomes much easier. Reading the Bible is not an obligation but a privileged way to access the heart of God. Look for him in the pages, the stories, the poetry, the letters you read in his Word. Listen and allow him to speak to your heart through Scripture, nourishing your spirit, healing your wounds, comforting you, instructing you, and empowering you, for as Hebrews 4:12 reminds us, "The Word of God is alive and active."

SECTION 2

FIND FREEDOM

*F*reedom.

The word always makes me think of William Wallace and *Braveheart*, the award-winning film based on Wallace's epic stand against King Edward I of England in the First War of Scottish Independence at the end of the thirteenth century. When I think about freedom, I recall the unforgettable scene where Wallace tries to rouse his fellow Scots to battle.

He asks the large crowd, "What will you do?"

They look up and consider the daunting size of the English army and shout, "We will run!"

It's funny for us today, at least for the briefest of moments, but then Wallace responds with a profound truth that's no laughing matter. He says, "Run and you'll live—at least a while. And dying in your beds, many years from now, would you be willing to trade all the days from this day to that for one chance, just one chance, to come back here and tell our enemies that they may take our lives, but they'll never take our freedom!"

I'm convinced that every human being wants to be free, to enjoy the ability to choose for themselves where and how they live out their lives. This inherent longing for freedom motivated the patriots who formed our nation and the many men and women who have died defending our country's freedom ever since.

It's in us to be free—God put the longing there. But the enemy of our souls wants us to run, to hide from conflict, and to avoid fighting for whom we were made to be. Yet once we have a relationship with God, we have his power in us. We don't have to face life's challenges alone. Our fears, anxieties, and worries cannot enslave us. The enemy's snares no longer leave us trapped, victims of circumstances beyond our control.

Once we begin our relationship with God, once we start getting to know him and walking with him daily, the next step in our journey is allowing his power to transform and heal us, to set us free. The power of our relationship with our loving Father changes us, providing us with the courage, strength, and resilience we need to face old wounds, ongoing hang-ups, and destructive attitudes.

The theological term for this step is *deliverance*, which can sound dramatic and scary but is usually subtler and more gradual. We may think we'll experience some spectacular moment, like a scene out of *The Exorcist*, when we're instantly healed and unburdened from all our struggles; that can and does happen sometimes, but typically that's not how it works.

Instead, we often must face the painful scars of our past and invite God to heal us in those areas. We have to take responsibility for our habits and behaviors and the sinful ways we may be trying to get our personal needs met. For most people, deliverance comes down to a specific, challenging area of their lives that continues to have a grip on them.

This struggle is not a heaven-or-hell issue—the blood of Jesus has already taken care of that. No, this battle is a quality-of-life issue, a matter of how we will live out our earthly lives until we get to heaven. The enemy would love to keep us distracted, distressed, and depressed over this struggle so that we never grow and reach our full potential, doing all that God has called us to do.

Chances are good you know exactly what I'm talking about.

It's that one area that keeps holding you back. The same request that's almost always in your prayers. The constant goal that shows up each year in your resolutions. The secret you're afraid to share.

The place where you most need freedom.

FREEDOM FOR THE PRISONERS

Freedom is one of the major reasons Jesus came to earth, to live and die and rise again in his defeat of the enemy once and for all. When Jesus began his public ministry, he went to the synagogue and read the words of the prophet Isaiah:

> "The Spirit of the Lord is on me, because he has anointed me to proclaim good news to the poor. He has sent me to proclaim freedom for the prisoners and

recovery of sight for the blind, to set the oppressed
free, to proclaim the year of the Lord's favor." (Luke
4:18–19)

Christ came to preach the good news of the gospel,
and that's the first step—restoring our relationship with
God as we receive and experience his grace and love in
our salvation. But the next step is living fully in this new
spiritual realm of complete freedom. We see evidence of
this frequently, as Jesus delivered people throughout his
ministry, "how God anointed Jesus of Nazareth with the
Holy Spirit and power, and how he went around doing
good and healing all who were under the power of the
devil, because God was with him" (Acts 10:38). We're
also told, "The reason the Son of God appeared was to
destroy the devil's work" (1 John 3:8).

What's interesting is that most of us are not bound
as tightly as we think we are. Most of our issues stem
from the lies we've accepted as truth that cause us to stay
where we are, stuck in place, running on a treadmill of
repetitive negative thoughts that prevent us from moving forward in God's freedom. We think there's nothing
we can do to change—which is true, *we* can't—but our
God can!

If you want to take the next step in your spiritual
growth, then it's time to break free from the chains that
bind you and the obstacles that continually seem to trip
you up. God's Word tells us how:

For though we live in the world, we do not wage war as the world does. The weapons we fight with are not the weapons of the world. On the contrary, they have divine power to demolish strongholds. We demolish arguments and every pretension that sets itself up against the knowledge of God, and we take captive every thought to make it obedient to Christ. (2 Corinthians 10:3–5)

The word *strongholds* comes from the Greek *ochyroma*, which literally means a prisoner locked up by deception or, in other words, living life by some belief that is not true. I like Beth Moore's strategy for overcoming these false beliefs. In her book *Praying God's Word*, she teaches how to pray Scripture to overcome the enemy's strongholds. She defines a stronghold as anything that exalts itself in our minds, "pretending" to be bigger or more powerful than our God.[1] The issue, struggle, or secret is not bigger or more powerful than our ability to overcome it, but too often we think it is.

LIES THAT BIND

Living life based on a pervasive false belief reminds me of the story of Elizabeth Smart. You may recall she was abducted at age fourteen from her home in Salt Lake City by a man named Brian David Mitchell. Assisted by his wife, Wanda Barzee, Mitchell held young Elizabeth Smart captive for nine months until she was rescued by authorities on a street in Sandy, Utah—less than twenty miles from her home.

As Smart's story during her captivity unfolded, it was clear that she could have escaped several times before she was recognized by neighbors in Sandy who contacted the police. Smart's abductor often took her out in public, veiled or disguised, and even to the local library once. During one such outing, the police stopped them and asked them if they had seen a local girl gone missing named Elizabeth Smart.

Standing right in front of them, all she had to do was shout, "I am Elizabeth Smart!"—and yet she did not. Fed lies by her abductors, Smart was convinced something bad would happen if she told the truth about her identity. She thought Mitchell and his wife would hurt not only her but also her family. Her fear of something that wasn't true kept her from being free.

This is how the devil operates. He has power in this world but no authority. So, he keeps talking to us until we believe him. We end up accepting his lies as truth, letting them into our thoughts so that they poison our emotions and influence our actions. Satan pretends that he has authority over us—but this is not true. We have been given authority through the power of Jesus Christ and his Spirit who dwells in us. But too often we don't own and exercise the authority and power we've been given. Instead, we believe a lie and empower the liar.

We all experience these strongholds and their impact on our lives. They steal our focus and begin to consume our minds. They make us feel controlled by our desires and fears until we believe we're powerless to change. We start saying things like, "I will never be able to stop this. I will always be powerless when it comes to this."

Soon, this stronghold becomes a part of our identity. We focus only on our weakness, our failure, our struggle, our addiction. We reduce ourselves to only this as the center of our identities, saying, "I am a smoker. I am an alcoholic. I am an addict. I am a cheater. I am a liar. I am an adulterer. I will always fail."

Satan loves when we imprison ourselves this way. He wants us to internalize our addictions so that his lies become part of our thinking, preventing us from knowing the truth of our freedom in Christ. Soon, his lies are so ingrained that we begin to make excuses for ourselves and justify giving in to temptations again and again.

This cycle consumes emotional energy. We feel increasingly hopeless. Our lives seem like one big failure, one constant battle, without a moment's peace. We become convinced there's no way out.

And that's exactly what the enemy wants—to distract us from our God-given purpose and the power God has given us to live out this purpose. Satan's ultimate goal is to keep us from being effective. He comes to steal and kill and destroy. He wants to rob us of the abundant life Jesus came to bring. But we don't have to stand idly by and let him win.

YOUR BRAVE HEART

Overcoming strongholds and living in freedom is so essential to the Christian life that our church has created an entire ministry around it. We have Freedom small groups and encourage everyone in our Highlands family to experience them once they've accepted Jesus as their Savior and started their spiritual journey. In these community-based small groups, our people go through a twelve-week curriculum that exposes the many lies they may believe and replaces them with God's truth. Layer by layer, the enemy's lies are revealed, strongholds are overcome, and healing begins. We have assurance from God's Word that "they will come to their senses and escape from the trap of the devil, who has taken them captive to do his will" (2 Timothy 2:26).

So, specifically, how do we break free? What does this process of living in freedom look like? That's what this section is all about.

"When a strong man, armed to the teeth, stands guard in his front yard, his property is safe and sound. But what if a stronger man comes along with superior weapons? Then he's beaten at his own game, the arsenal that gave him such confidence hauled off, and his precious possessions plundered." (Luke 11:21–22 THE MESSAGE)

I want you to be strong, equipped, empowered. In the words of William Wallace, I want you to accept God's invitation: "Your heart is free. Have the courage to follow it."

CHAPTER FOUR

RELATIONSHIPS

SHOW ME YOUR FRIENDS

My preaching will never change anyone's life. It's painfully disappointing to admit, but I know it's true. And here's how I can prove it: if you talk to any member or regular attender at our church and ask them to describe the last five messages I've preached, I'd be surprised if they could name more than one—if that! Even though they liked those sermons and benefited from them on the day I delivered them, the sermons themselves likely didn't create a lasting impression on most people's lives.

But everyone can name five people who have made a dramatic impact on their lives, for both good and bad. It might be an extended family member or a teacher, coach, or pastor. Maybe it's your best friend from high school, your boss at your first job, or your neighbor on the corner. I'll bet you can easily think of more than five in less than a minute, each one shaping you and influencing your life in some profound way.

Don't get me wrong—I love good preaching and do everything I can to facilitate the most worshipful, impactful church services possible. Preaching and teaching play important roles in the process of living in the full freedom of your identity in Christ. Hearing God's Word and learning his truth serve as powerful catalysts for your desire to change, even as they equip you to overcome the enemy's obstacles in your life.

But the real test occurs not on Sunday mornings or whenever you attend church, but day in and day out as you live, work, parent, drive, shop, cook, minister, and everything else you do on any given day. And you'll rarely have success living out your faith and exercising your spiritual freedom if it's just you and God. He made us in his own image as relational beings, so it's no surprise that change happens in us within the context of our relationships.

TRUE CONFESSIONS

Why is community so important in our process of living in freedom? It's not only about learning and growing together; it's about experiencing God's grace together. When we fall short of God's holy and perfect standard—when we sin—we confess our shortcomings to God and receive forgiveness. His Word tells us, "If we confess our sins, he is faithful and just and will forgive us our sins and purify us from all unrighteousness" (1 John 1:9).

Only God can forgive our sins, but confession takes care of what we did. It doesn't guarantee we won't mess up again. In fact, left to our own devices, most of us will fail time after time. But God provided a solution, a system that relies on our identity as relational beings. He said, "Therefore confess your sins to each other and pray for each other so that you may be healed" (James 5:16).

We confess our sins not only to God, but also to each other. This system provides spiritual support as we pray for one another and help one another, which facilitates healing. Notice the big picture here: we go to God for forgiveness, and we go to God's people for healing.

Surrounding ourselves with the right people is one of the most important steps in our spiritual journeys. When we develop relationships, get involved in each other's trials and triumphs, and basically do life together, we help each other grow and develop more spiritual muscle. We begin trusting each other and sharing honestly and openly instead of hiding behind the polite social customs we've been conditioned to uphold.

I can't tell you how many times I've asked someone at our church how they're doing, only to have them automatically reply, "Good. How are you, Pastor Chris?" Much of the time, I answer with the same response: "I'm fine. Good to see you!" I know we can't stop and have a heart-to-heart chat with every neighbor, coworker, friend, or church member we encounter. Nor would it be appropriate to share our deepest struggles and greatest concerns with just anyone. But if we're looking to walk fully in the freedom and healing God calls us to, we do need the support of a community of other believers moving in the same direction, God's direction.

Because we all face moments when we don't know how to keep going.

When our faith is stretched to the breaking point.

When we need the loving support of others to see us through.

WOOD ON THE FIRE

Everyone has been shaped by their relationships. Whether you realize it or not, you are the sum total of all the key relationships in your life up until now. All the more reason to pay close attention to your choice of friends. According to the Bible, "A mirror reflects a man's face, but what he is really like is shown by the kind of friends he chooses" (Proverbs 27:19 TLB). You are where you are because of your relationships.

Think about your life right now—your hopes and

dreams, your joys and accomplishments, as well as your disappointments and struggles, your fears and frustrations. Now consider the way your key relationships—those people you spend the most time with and invest the most energy in knowing—influence you. Some situations may be obvious, while others seem complex and require more consideration. But without a doubt, your relationships play a role in some of the most important decisions you'll ever make. As you think about the relationships in your life, I encourage you to make four crucial choices.

1. FOCUS ON NURTURING THE RELATIONSHIPS THAT ARE MOST IMPORTANT TO YOU.

For many people, this means spouses, children, and other close loved ones. I'm always moved by the number of people who request prayer for their troubled marriages through our prayer cards at church. Occasionally, I'm asked to counsel couples who feel like their marriage is broken. In these situations, often the first thing I tell them is that they have a better marriage than they think they do—otherwise, they wouldn't bother trying to improve it by coming to see me or by requesting prayer from others.

Nonetheless, one or both individuals typically say, "No, our marriage is terrible, Pastor. The fire has gone out. There's nothing left here. It's broken beyond repair."

"Just because the fire has gone out," I tell them, "doesn't mean you can't restart it. Don't blame the fireplace just because you're cold! For the fireplace to work, you have to put wood on it—continuously." Good marriages, and strong relationships of any kind, require maintenance and nurturing. Your marriage is as good as you want it to be, really.

Many people complain about the quality of their most important relationships yet do little to nurture them. They neglect to invest their time, attention, and energy and then wonder why their needs aren't being met by the other person. Your spouse needs to know they're second only to God in your relationships. Your children need to know you love them even when you don't always like what they do or how they do it.

If your relationships aren't where you want them to be, try nurturing them. You can't grow in your faith by walking alone. You need the love, support, and accountability that come from Christian community.

2. CHOOSE TO RESTORE THE BROKEN RELATIONSHIPS IN YOUR LIFE.

All of us have relationships that go bad, sometimes due to our own fault and sometimes the other person's, but usually a broken relationship is the result of two sinful people hurting each other. Often, your pride and ego refuse to budge—after all, your sister is the one who said all those things about you, so why should you forgive her when she won't take responsibility for her offense? But here's something to think about: the pain of unresolved conflict is greater than the pain required to resolve it.

The old saying is true. When you hold a grudge and won't forgive someone, you poison yourself, not the other person. The best gift you can give yourself is to forgive anyone who has wounded you in some way. You can't force someone else to apologize, ask for forgiveness, or repent, but you can control how you respond in your own heart before the Lord. The Bible makes this clear: "Do not repay anyone evil for evil. . . . If it is possible, as far as it depends on you, live at peace with everyone" (Romans 12:17–18).

If you're unable to talk to the other person face-to-face—perhaps they won't speak to you or live thousands of miles away, or maybe they've even passed away—you can still choose to forgive them in your heart. Your heart should reflect God's heart, which keeps no record of our offenses (Psalm 130:3–4).

When you choose to forgive someone—and notice I keep stressing *choose*, which means you do it even if you don't feel like doing it—then you hold nothing against them. You turn the matter over to God and no longer have to worry about it. Such release comes easier when you consider how much God has forgiven you. And the Bible reminds us that there is a direct relationship between these two things: "Bear with each other and forgive one another if any of you has a grievance against someone. Forgive as the Lord forgave you" (Colossians 3:13).

In the model of the Lord's Prayer, Jesus told us to choose forgiveness as we remember how much we've been forgiven. Forgiveness is one of the healthiest habits we can practice as we lean into community and the deepening of our faith. When we forgive others and ask forgiveness from the people we've offended, we liberate ourselves from bitterness, resentment, and vengeance.

3. KNOW WHEN TO WALK AWAY.

No matter how much or how often you've forgiven someone, sometimes you must sever your relationship with them. Just because you forgive them doesn't mean you must continue to interact with them. Some relationships are so harmful and toxic that you simply must walk away and maintain a firm boundary. Otherwise, the person will continue to hurt you and undermine your faith.

Just to be clear, I am not talking about divorcing a spouse on unbiblical grounds. Don't twist this practice into something convenient for you that doesn't reflect what God wants. Just because someone frustrates you or makes your life uncomfortable does not mean you should walk away.

No, I'm talking about harmful relationships. The ones that batter your heart, soul, mind, and body with ongoing abuse, stress, pain, and deception. Sometimes you may choose not to sever the relationship, but you can at least redefine it.

Evaluating your friendships is critical to your spiritual growth and well-being. Show me your friends, and I'll show you your future. "Walk with the wise and become wise, for a companion of fools suffers harm" (Proverbs 13:20).

Some people are in unholy relationships, such as cohabitating outside of marriage, yet they wonder why they're not growing spiritually. Or they continue to hang out with ungodly friends who like to drink and party, because they're afraid of walking away and cultivating new friendships with other believers. They want to belong to their old group even though they know how the group behaves isn't good for them. The Bible says, "Do not be misled: 'Bad company corrupts good character'" (1 Corinthians 15:33).

How can you know which relationships you should leave behind? It's simple, really. If a relationship hinders your relationship with God, then you need to either redefine it or sever it.

4. RISK BEING REAL.

Take the risk to initiate some meaningful relationships in your life. Probably the best way to practice this habit is to build on some of the relationships and friendships you already have, perhaps with others from your small group, a trusted friend in your Bible study, or a prayer partner in your old neighborhood.

Pray for the right opportunity and find time to get together in person when you won't be rushed or glued to your phone. Then share what's going on in your heart—your concerns, your fears, your worries—and ask this person to pray for you. Invite them to open themselves up to you in the same way. Discuss ways you can encourage each other throughout the week or until you're able to meet and pray together again in person. Sometimes a brief text, email, or call from a trusted friend can remind you of God's power to get you through a tough day.

You need to realize, though, that all of hell will try to stop you. The enemy doesn't want you forming strong, meaningful relationships that both draw you closer to God and deepen your faith. Expect your attempts to connect with others to be difficult at times. You may think it's easier to not even try. But remember what God's Word says: "[Let us not give] up meeting together, as some are in the habit of doing, but [let us encourage] one another—and all the more as you see the Day approaching" (Hebrews 10:25).

In our world of social media updates about our latest purchase or next vacation, letting someone into the messiness of your life can be scary. But I'm convinced that if you get real, you'll get some real friends.

Don't worry what others will think of you or let your fears prevent you from being open and honest. You've worn the mask for long enough. Each of us is recovering from something that has changed us—we will all show some nicks and scrapes once our walls come down—but knowing that you're not the only one, that others are struggling with the same issues and feelings, can feel remarkably liberating.

If you're willing to be real with others, you might be surprised what you'll discover:

Friends who walk in when everyone else walks out.
Friends who don't rub it in but help you work it out.
Friends who need you as much as you need them.

RELATIONAL AREAS

If you're not sure how to cultivate more meaningful relationships, let me encourage you to consider three areas where you can practice.

CHURCH

The first area is simply a church community. You need a church home that can support you in your faith as well as give you opportunities to serve others with the gifts God has given you. I'm not about to tell you which kind of church to seek out—let the Holy Spirit guide you there—only that you need to be part of some family of believers. As Paul reminds us, "You are members of God's very own family . . . and you belong in God's household with every other Christian" (Ephesians 2:19 TLB).

At Church of the Highlands where I pastor, we have many members, as well as regular attenders and visitors. We welcome everyone, but I generally recommend that those who attend should only do so for a while before committing or moving on to find another church where they can commit. I encourage you to do the same. There's no set length of time you should attend a church before committing; this is more about your attitude in relationship to your church.

It's easy to simply attend a church, enjoying the worship service and fellowship week after week. But membership involves privileges—and responsibilities— that regular attendance doesn't. Membership requires commitment: *I need you and you need me, so let's commit to being in this spiritual family together.*

If you don't believe me, then I challenge you to commit to the church you've been attending for one year and watch the difference. Commitment always builds character. You will experience your relationships within the church differently when you—and others—know you're committed to being there.

Committing to your church creates opportunities to cultivate deeper, stronger friendships with others who want to grow closer to God. We see this pattern throughout the early days of the church, as described in the New Testament. Followers of Jesus would meet in someone's home or in a secluded area outdoors and worship together. They would read God's Word, and often someone would teach or preach. They would fellowship together, talking and eating and enjoying the encouragement that comes from being together: "All the believers met together constantly and shared everything with each other" (Acts 2:44 TLB).

The key, as we see in this verse, involves sharing everything together—being real and doing life together.

TEAM

If you want to cultivate more meaningful relationships, then another area to get involved in is a team of some sort. Teams require you to work together with other individuals to produce greater results than any one person could achieve alone. When you serve with a group of others who share your same passion or specific interest, you may be surprised how fun it can be. Sure, it's usually hard work, but doing it together makes a difference.

Some of the happiest, most fulfilled people I know tell me their secret is serving on a team. They feel part of a group that's making a difference. They share a commitment with their team members to live out the purpose or objective of their team. Knowing they make a difference for those around them—as well as those they serve alongside—produces a sense of lasting joy.

Again, don't be surprised if the enemy undermines your attempts to be part of a team. He'll lie to you and tell you that you don't need others and that you're better off alone. He'll try to convince you that it's better to do things your way instead of compromising for the sake of the team. But the devil is wrong! The Bible says, "There was a man all alone; he had neither son nor brother. There was no end to his toil, yet his eyes were not content with his wealth. . . . Two are better than one, because they have a good return for their labor" (Ecclesiastes 4:8–9).

Our enemy knows that emotional and spiritual healing often happens in community, which in turn sustains our ability to live in the freedom Christ gives us. When we belong to a group of other people with whom we can be honest and vulnerable, we grow as we love, challenge, correct, and support one another. We can remind each other of God's truth to combat the lies the devil tries to use against us.

GOD

Finally, if you want deeper, more meaningful relationships with others that lead to freedom, cultivate your relationship with God. I know we already covered this earlier, but don't become so focused on connecting with other people that you neglect your primary relationship. Remember, Jesus is not only your Savior and Lord; he's your friend.

In fact, Christ commanded us in the same passage to love God with all our hearts and to love other people. During his time on earth, Jesus made it clear we can't really love God without loving people. And we can't love people without loving God. Both are necessary.

We go to God for forgiveness.

We go to God's people for healing.

YOUR NEXT STEP ON THE JOURNEY

In the Old Testament we're told that temple priests wore names over their hearts. Their holy garments included breastplates inscribed with the names of the tribes of Israel, as well as the various names of God. The ritual symbolized the way both God and other people came together within the hearts of those serving the Lord.

We don't have to wear articles of clothing or armor with others' names physically inscribed on them, but I've found that most of us still have names over our hearts—the names of those individuals who have shaped us, loved us, nurtured us, and helped us grow in our faith. Among the names inscribed on my heart is Billy Hornsby, my father-in-law.

Billy was so much more than just a father-in-law to me—he was a mentor, friend, confidant, and brother in Christ. I could write an entire book about the many ways Billy poured into my life and made me a better man and a stronger Christian. Although Billy has passed from this life and is now with the Lord, not a day goes by that I don't miss him or appreciate how he enriched my life. His name is on my heart forever.

Whose name is over your heart?

Make a list of the people inscribed on your heart. Then spend a few moments in prayer for each one. Give God thanks for the joy, instruction, and wisdom these individuals add to your life.

CHAPTER FIVE

TRANSPARENCY

HONESTY IS THE BEST POLICY

As a father of five, I know a thing or two about honesty—as well as how to spot *dis*honesty. When our kids were small, Tammy and I worked hard to teach them that we didn't expect them to be perfect, but we did expect them to be honest. Surprisingly enough, they sometimes reminded us that they were listening.

I'll never forget the time when I came home from work and found the beginnings of someone's wood-carving career in our bedroom. We still lived in Louisiana at the time, where I was on staff as an associate pastor at my home church. I came home after a long day and couldn't wait to get out of my dress clothes and into something more comfortable.

After tossing my jacket on the bed, I removed my button-down shirt and hung it on the bedpost while I finished changing. Only, the bedpost looked like the remains of a woodpecker's lunch. Our beautiful solid-wood bed with its old-fashioned headboard, footboard, and four spindled posts looked like the victim of a back-alley mugging. Deep gouges in the dark hickory wood competed with long gashes in a random pattern on the corner post beside me. Wood chips and sawdust littered the comforter and floor all around the corner of the bed.

My blood pressure immediately jumped several digits as I yelled out, "Unbelievable! Okay, who did this?" Realizing no one heard me, I finished changing, grabbed my whistle, and stood in our living room. Like Captain von Trapp in *The Sound of Music*, I gave the "all come" signal, five short bursts that meant everyone should stop what they were doing and gather immediately. Kids clambered from the other rooms in our house and lined up in front of me, curious to know what was going on.

Knowing my kids—and it's amazing how quickly their distinct little personalities emerge—I had a good idea who the culprit was. Our son David, who was probably around seven at the time, had been a handful from the time he began crawling, always getting into things, pushing limits, seeing what he could get away with, doing things he knew he shouldn't do just to see what would happen. He had already proved himself to be the child who would keep his parents on their knees. This crime had his fingerprints all over it.

"Someone carved up the bedpost in Mommy and Daddy's bedroom," I said calmly, but with a little anger and paternal authority sprinkled on top. "Anyone know who did this? I have a good idea, so you might as well go ahead and tell me now." My eyes locked onto David's as he gazed defiantly back at me. The other kids gasped, and my daughter looked like she would cry.

Jonathan, around five at the time, raised his hand and smiled sheepishly. "I know, Daddy," he said. "I did it!"

For a moment you could hear the proverbial pin drop.

Of all our children, Jonathan would have been the least likely to do something like this. He's our fourth child and third son and has since been described as the nicest of us Hodges. Jonathan has a kind heart. He's easygoing and gentle in his approach to the world. I was shocked to think of him going at the bedpost like Norman Bates at a shower curtain.

"*You* carved up our bedpost, Jonathan?" I asked.

He nodded vigorously and kept smiling, a sweet, mischievous twinkle in his eye.

"Why would you do that, buddy?"

He shrugged. "I don't know."

His immediate transparency totally disarmed me. I had to suppress a chuckle as I sensed some of his innocent joy in disclosing what he'd done. This was not how I expected the scene to play out. I dismissed the kids and told Jonathan that his mother and I would tell him his punishment after dinner. By bedtime, I had decided not to discipline him at all as a reward for his candor. Jonathan's honesty was unexpected, attractive, and disarming. Because he was so honest, I immediately wanted to forgive him.

I also gained new insight into why God asks us to be honest with him.

God doesn't expect perfection.

He just wants honesty.

TROUBLE IN PARADISE

From the beginning of creation, God has asked for honesty—not perfection. I suppose it was easy for Adam and Eve to be honest with God at first, because they had not yet disobeyed him. They had no secrets or hidden agendas, only full transparency with each other and with God. But after they ate the fruit from the Tree of Knowledge of Good and Evil, they immediately wanted to cover up their shame, both literally with fig leaves and figuratively by hiding from God.

Adam and Eve, of course, are not the only ones who tried to hide from God and cover up their sin. After David committed adultery by sleeping with Bathsheba, he tried to cover it up by having her husband killed. Finally, with the help of God's prophet Nathan, David came to his senses, confessed his sin, and repented before God. Expressing his repentant heart in Psalm 51, David observed, "For I was born a sinner—yes, from the moment my mother conceived me. But you desire honesty from the womb, teaching me wisdom even there" (Psalm 51:5–6 NLT).

Another version of Scripture translates "honesty from the womb" as "truth in the inward parts" (Psalm 51:6 NKJV) to reinforce this truth. No matter how we express it, though, the requirement is the same: God requires complete and utter openness and honesty from his children. He knows that because he has given us free will to choose, we have a choice about not only what we do, but also who and what and how we tell about what we've done. Because he is a holy God of complete and absolute truth, he desires and requires truth from us.

With our sinful nature activated by Adam's and Eve's sin back in the Garden, we all tend to create our own fig leaves and cover up our mistakes and indiscretions. We don't want to face the truth about what we've done and the impact our selfishness has had on others. We don't want to own up to the consequences of our actions or face the punishment that comes with disobedience. It's so much easier to hide—from ourselves, from others, from God—and refuse to engage with the truth.

However, if we want to live in the fullness of God's freedom, we must commit to living in truth. Jesus told his followers, "If you hold to my teaching, you are really my disciples. Then you will know the truth, and the truth will set you free" (John 8:31–32). Facing the truth is not always easy or comfortable, but it's the only way to grow closer to God and to mature in our faith. As Jesus said, it's the only way to be free.

At our church we like to say that you're only as sick as your secrets—whatever you're hiding, running from, denying. It could be an addiction, a mistake from your past, an ongoing battle with gossip or shopping or gambling—whatever destructive habit consumes your time, energy, and attention and pulls you away from God. You probably feel deep shame. You likely have regrets. You may feel trapped and unsure of how to get unstuck.

But the answer is simple, really.

Face the truth.

Tell the truth.

Accept God's truth.

BURYING THE TRUTH

King David had secrets—certainly his affair with Bathsheba was a big one—but he also had an incredibly intimate relationship with God. I'm fascinated by the way God was so merciful to David, arguably showing the shepherd-boy-turned-king more grace than other figures in Scripture. What was David's secret? What did he do that God liked so much? Why did God call David "a man after my own heart" (Acts 13:22)?

Here's my theory: David's relationship with God was deep and intimate because he was honest, transparent, and quick to repent. If we return to the psalm he wrote after his sin with Bathsheba, we see it's clearly a prayer of repentance. He begins by simply asking God to have mercy on him, acknowledging his sin outright—not just his adultery but his very nature from birth—along with his awareness that God desires the truth (Psalm 51:6).

So many people never find freedom because they're committed to concealing the truth. They work hard to hide from it because it feels too uncomfortable, too painful, too humbling to face. Rather than acknowledge the truth before God, they choose to handle their past mistakes, current problems, and secret hang-ups themselves.

Have you ever found yourself going this route? You put your sin in a box, lock it up, and shove it deep into the recesses of your heart. Or you sweep it under the rug, constantly fighting to keep it from crawling out again. You can try to bury it, but here's the problem: it doesn't stay buried. It's like trying to hold a beach ball under the surface of the water. Momentarily invisible, it can be held underwater only so long before it shoots up and breaks the surface again for all to see.

What does this look like in our everyday lives? It's when we minimize an unpleasant truth and tell ourselves, "It's no big deal. It's not so bad." Of course, if that were true, then why does it still bother us? Why does it linger in our minds?

Or it's when we rationalize the truth about our sinful mistakes. "Nobody's perfect. This isn't as bad as what others have done." While this may be true—we can always find someone who has made either better or worse choices than ourselves—it doesn't let us off the hook. Justification of our wrong choices becomes nothing more than a temporary smokescreen.

It could also be when we try to bury the truth by compromising. "If you feel bad about what you did yesterday, then just lower your standards," which leads to "I'm a bad person, and that's just the way it is." Pretty soon, as we lower our expectations for our life, for our future, we find ourselves growing cynical and hard-hearted. Such a bitter mindset causes us to beat ourselves up. We begin living in the land of regret, always looking in the rearview mirror of our lives, missing out on the present moment and all God has for us. Whether consciously or subconsciously, we administer self-punishment. We condemn ourselves and feel even worse. "No one will love me if they know who I really am and what I've done. There's no way anyone could forgive me."

Despite how quickly he usually repented, David also went down this dead-end path a time or two. In another psalm, he wrote, "My guilt has overwhelmed me like a burden too heavy to bear. My wounds fester and are loathsome because of my sinful folly. . . . I am feeble and utterly crushed; I groan in anguish of heart" (Psalm 38:4–5, 8).

The weight of our secrets can crush us, especially if

we're piling on self-contempt, shame, and condemnation. Sometimes this burden manifests itself physically in the form of an illness or chronic condition. For example, I suspect depression can be a form of self-inflicted punishment in certain situations. We sin in some way and bury the truth, leading us to expect the worst and feel like that's all we deserve. Set up for failure, we create a self-fulfilling prophecy. "I don't deserve to succeed," we tell ourselves.

Sometimes, though, instead of internalizing the truth of our sinful mistakes, we blame others. This is a well-known, timeless tactic. In fact, this strategy is as old as creation! Going back to Adam and Eve, we see them blaming each other as well as being the first to point out, "The devil made me do it!" Eve told God, "The serpent deceived me, and I ate" (Genesis 3:13). In other words, "It's not my fault!"

Whether we admit it or not, we all like to blame others—myself included. We accuse others and excuse ourselves. We're victims of circumstances beyond our control. We pass the buck and slip into the victim mindset, which often sends us deeper into denial—and farther away from the truth and freedom God desires for us.

LOOK OUT THE WINDOW

There is a much better way of handling the truth about our weaknesses, mistakes, and sinful choices. The remedy is simple but challenging. If we want to live in the freedom of the truth, we must practice brutal honesty. We do this when we share our authentic selves with others. This kind of authenticity results in both a deeper personal relationship with God, as we grow increasingly aware of his grace in our lives, and deeper relationships with those around us as they see reflected in us the power of the Holy Spirit to change lives. Developing full transparency and healthy intimacy requires practice.

One of the best tools I know, and one we use at our church frequently, is a technique called the Johari Window. Developed by psychologists Joseph Luft and Harrington Ingham in 1955, this exercise helps us understand ourselves and others with greater clarity. In it, we look at four areas or quadrants of knowledge: what you and others both know, what you know but they don't, what they know but you don't, and what neither can know. Let's take a quick look at each area.

THE FIRST PANE OF THE JOHARI WINDOW, OFTEN CALLED THE ARENA, REFLECTS THE KNOWLEDGE WE ALL KNOW.

This is the public "you," the one others see in your day-to-day life. It can be tempting to cultivate your image a certain way, and with social media, this temptation is greater than ever. Sure, you want others to know about your latest accomplishment or next great vacation. There's nothing wrong with wanting to share the most positive, publicly laudable aspects of who you are; the problem is when this surface version is the only dimension of you people ever know.

THE SECOND PANE OF THE WINDOW IS WHAT WE KNOW, BUT OTHERS DON'T.

This quadrant reveals the tension between the way others see us (and the way we think they see us) and how we see ourselves. We all wear masks, often becoming who we think those around us want or need us to be. Other times, we put on masks that we think will help us get what we want from others.

The problem with masks, though, is that when we wear them long enough, we forget who we really are beneath them. Masks help us cling to denial and pretend that everything's okay, when deep inside we know it's not. We all have secrets, but you're in trouble if you're the only one who knows them. Again, you will always be as sick as your secrets.

One of the most destructive lies the enemy whispers to our hearts is that we must not let others see who we really are. So, we build walls and create elaborate defense systems to appear the way we think we should be and hide the real person we are on the inside. But living in this kind of solitary confinement is not only lonely; it kills our hearts. We all long to be seen and known by others. If we want deeper, life-changing relationships with others, then transparency and honesty are essential.

THE THIRD PANE OF THE WINDOW IS WHAT OTHERS KNOW THAT WE DON'T KNOW ABOUT OURSELVES.

To overcome your own limitations and weaknesses, you need trustworthy people willing to tell you what they see that you cannot see. We all have blind spots. It's like having body odor or spinach in your teeth—everyone knows it but you! You see this lack of self-awareness in many different forms, including the entertainment world.

Think about all those people who audition for shows like *American Idol* who literally can't carry a note in a bucket, as my granddaddy used to say. They sound terrible but apparently don't realize it themselves. They think they're the next big pop superstar. When the judges burst their bubble by telling them the truth, it's painful, to say the least. They realize not only that they cannot sing, but also that they don't have any real friends. Because if they did, those friends wouldn't have let them audition on national TV!

The same is true for you and me. We can't see our own blind spots. That's why we can't be the only set of eyes we rely on for perspective. In fact, when we're going through a tough time, our view may be so skewed by circumstances that we can't see clearly or objectively. In such situations, we're the last person whose judgment we should trust! After all, the Bible tells us, "The heart is deceitful above all things and beyond cure" (Jeremiah 17:9).

The truth is, we often can't see things as they really

are; we see things as *we* are. We need loving eyes to inform us of what we're missing. All the more reason to make sure we receive information about our blind spots from people we love and trust. Scripture reminds us, "Wounds from a friend can be trusted" (Proverbs 27:6).

Give some trusted individuals permission to speak into your life where you have blind spots. Be that kind of friend to them in return.

THE FOURTH PANE OF THE WINDOW IS WHAT NEITHER WE NOR OTHER PEOPLE KNOW.

There are things I don't know and you don't know—only God knows. Consequently, we bond by discovering together what God wants to reveal to us as we step out in faith and grow into the future. God designed intimacy to be experiential and not just based on shared knowledge. Each of us contributes uniquely to our growth together within the body of Christ. "He makes the whole body fit together perfectly. As each part does its own special work, it helps the other parts grow" (Ephesians 4:16 NLT).

The Johari Window provides us with a concise, effective way of evaluating our relationships with others. There's nothing special or supernatural about it. Simply using it as a tool, though, can remind us of some important truths about the ways we relate to others. Foremost, we need to dig beyond the surface. This means we will need to share what often feels too scary to let anyone else know. We need to listen to trusted individuals who see what we can't see in ourselves. And we need to be open to learning together to maximize the power of honesty in our lives.

You'll never know what your full potential is until you connect with others at a deep, honest level. You cannot connect without being intimate. *We* is always better than *me*.

YOUR NEXT STEP ON THE JOURNEY

No matter where you may be, take the next step toward living in freedom by investing extra time and attention into relationships with others who share your values, love you, and love God. They may be from your small group at church, your neighborhood, your apartment building, or your mother's-day-out program. Be honest with them. Ask them to be accountability partners with you. Tell them you need their help so you can grow.

I know firsthand how powerful this kind of honesty in a relationship can be. You may recall that prayer is a bit of a struggle for me sometimes. During a particularly dry spell, I once had one of my closest friends, who was also a pastor, meet me every morning for three weeks. Every day at 6 a.m., we met and then went into separate rooms for an hour to pray. Knowing I had to meet him and that he, too, was praying while I was praying made a huge difference. He came alongside me and helped me become a stronger prayer warrior.

As the Bible tells us, two are better than one—especially if the other person knows what you're really facing. If you want to live in freedom, share the truth with others and listen as they share the truth with you.

CHAPTER SIX

THE HOLY SPIRIT

A BREATH OF FRESH AIR

By the time I was fifteen, I had checked out on God. Then, as I mentioned earlier, a buddy invited me to a youth service at his church. The difference between his church and what I was used to experiencing on Sundays could not have been more distinct. Everyone in the service seemed genuinely happy and excited to be there, praising God and worshipping together. The teaching was not a must-do list or a don't-do list but application from the Bible that seemed directly relevant to my life. The other teens and young adults were taking notes, writing in their Bibles, nodding in agreement, clearly engaged in what the pastor was sharing.

I had never seen anything like it!

Their experience was so different that I wondered if it was real. And if this was who God *really* was, then I wanted to know him as they did. God wasn't keeping a checklist, marking down what I was doing and not doing; he just wanted to *know* me. My relationship with God, not my religion, determined where I would spend eternity. With this new realization, I prayed and invited Jesus into my heart, promising to give him control over all areas of my life.

While I knew I now had a personal relationship with the living God, and while I understood and accepted that Christ died on the cross for my sins, it wasn't long before I once again felt frustrated. Something was still missing. I felt like I'd been given the keys to a new car that had no gas in it.

Maybe a part of me knew what was missing was the Holy Spirit. But I was wary of unleashing his power in my life. In fact, I can remember praying, much to my embarrassment now, that the Holy Spirit would keep a low profile. I didn't want to be one of those out-of-control people shouting and singing and speaking in tongues, the kind of people we had looked down on in my hometown church.

Despite my defensive fears about unleashing the Spirit, I eventually found myself visiting a small group where the Holy Spirit was the main topic. While it was hard to sift through old prejudices and recycled rumors,

I decided once and for all to learn the truth about God's Spirit. I was determined to fully surrender and let the Spirit do anything and everything he wanted to do in my life. I wanted to be set free.

After I opened my heart to him, I was changed for the better in a bold, dramatic way. I became an on-fire believer who couldn't get enough of God's Word and who had to talk about Jesus with almost everyone he met. Instead of being uncomfortable and too embarrassed to discuss my faith with my friends, I suddenly started conversations that always led directly to Christ.

Best of all, I wasn't having to fake it or act the part of a good Christian. I could be myself and let the Holy Spirit penetrate my heart, my mind, and all areas of my life. Finally, I began to experience the exciting adventure of living out my faith. I not only had the keys to the new car I'd been given, I had a full tank that always overflowed!

WHEN THE SPIRIT MOVES

After I gave the Holy Spirit control over my life, I grew spiritually in leaps and bounds. In addition to reading my Bible more and talking to my friends about Jesus, I began to lead them to the Lord. I also began to lead prayer meetings and Bible studies. My fear and timidity had been transformed by the power and boldness of the Spirit.

Peter experienced this same kind of dramatic change. He went from being the guy who denied even knowing Jesus—not once but *three* times—to becoming an evangelist, the rock of the church, willing to die for his faith. What made the difference? Peter, like the other followers of Jesus at Pentecost (Acts 2), received the gift their Master had promised them—his Holy Spirit, a comforter and friend, a power source and breath of new life.

Not long after I invited the Holy Spirit to take control of my life, I was at a summer church camp. Along with several friends and several hundred other young adults, I was there at the Paul B. Johnson State Park to enjoy the outdoors and grow closer to God. Early in the week, we all gathered in an outdoor amphitheater to hear one of the staff members teach and preach. He was just about to conclude when he suddenly looked directly at me and called me to join him up front.

There, he told me the Holy Spirit had just given him a prophetic word about my life. "Look up, Chris," he said. "Do you see all the stars above us? Someday you will have a ministry that will reach more people than the number of stars you can count." He asked me to hold out my hands as a gesture of my willingness to receive what God had for me. Just as I extended my open palms, every finger on both hands popped. This had never happened before, and it has never happened since. It was like the Holy Spirit put an exclamation point on this experience!

Several years later, while I was visiting Birmingham

to attend a conference, I popped in to a Barnes & Noble for coffee since I had a few minutes to fill. Standing on the open patio sipping my latte, I stared out at the busy interstate just beyond the shopping center.

You see all those people driving by? the Spirit whispered to me. *Many of them will be part of the church you will start here.*

I wasn't surprised then, a few months later, when we founded Church of the Highlands less than a stone's throw from that very spot. And, appropriately, one of the foundational pillars of our church has always been reliance on the Holy Spirit. I'd experienced firsthand the power God wants to give us if we'll let him, and I wanted our church to be Spirit-fueled and Spirit-led. I like to tell people we embrace God's power without being weird about it!

THREE BAPTISMS

Why do I believe the Holy Spirit is such an essential part of knowing God and growing in your faith? Not because of my own experiences, but because God's Word says so. The Bible tells us there are three significant points when someone who accepts Jesus experiences the Holy Spirit. These three turning points are described as baptisms. While we usually think of baptism as a onetime event involving water, the word *baptism* actually means "immersion." Consequently, we are immersed in three different ways once we begin our new life in Christ.

1. BAPTISM OF SALVATION

When we give our hearts to Jesus, we're baptized into the body of Christ. We're immersed into his family, the church, and join our brothers and sisters in loving and serving God both individually and jointly. We're told, "By one Spirit we were all *baptized into one body*" (1 Corinthians 12:13 NKJV, my emphasis).

This is how the church started. This baptism occurred as Jesus' disciples received the Holy Spirit even before the Day of Pentecost:

> On the evening of that first day of the week, when the disciples were together, with the doors locked for fear of the Jewish leaders, Jesus came and stood among them and said, "Peace be with you!" After he said this, he showed them his hands and side. The disciples were overjoyed when they saw the Lord.
>
> Again Jesus said, "Peace be with you! As the Father has sent me, I am sending you." And with that he breathed on them and said, "*Receive the Holy Spirit.*" (John 20:19–22, my emphasis)

These disciples were the first people converted to what we now think of as Christianity. Based on their example, it's clear that we receive the Holy Spirit when we get saved. But there's more to their story, as we see when we consider other details from accounts of the same incident in the other Gospels.

In Luke's version we first find a similar description: "While they were still talking about this, Jesus himself stood among them and said to them, 'Peace be with you'" (Luke 24:36). Then, however, we're told something else Jesus said: "I am *going to* send you what my Father has promised; but stay in the city *until you have been clothed with power* from on high" (v. 49, my emphasis). Notice the future tense here, indicating this had not happened yet.

In Acts we find a similar account, yet with another striking detail:

> After his suffering, he presented himself to them and gave many convincing proofs that he was alive. He appeared to them over a period of forty days and spoke about the kingdom of God. On one occasion, while he was eating with them, he gave them this command: "Do not leave Jerusalem, but wait for the gift my Father promised, which you have heard me speak about. For John baptized with water, but *in a few days you will be baptized with the Holy Spirit*." (Acts 1:3–5, my emphasis)

Can you see the distinction? When you get saved, the Holy Spirit baptizes you into the body of Christ: "You are all children of God through faith, for all of you who were *baptized into Christ* have clothed yourselves with Christ" (Galatians 3:26–27, my emphasis). But another kind of baptism follows, an immersion separate from the one immediately occurring at salvation.

2. BAPTISM BY WATER

As discussed in chapter 1, water baptism is a public declaration of a private commitment. This immersion is a physical experience of being submerged in water and then rising from its surface, symbolizing the new life we have in Christ. We are buried with him and then participate through his Spirit in his resurrection to new life. Water washes us, cleansing our bodies and, symbolically, our spirits.

Many people ask me if you must have a water baptism to be saved. The answer, of course, is no. God's Word is clear: we are saved by grace, not by works (Ephesians 2:8–9). But the Bible is also clear that those who have been saved are to demonstrate their new identity symbolically: "Those who accepted [Peter's] message were baptized" (Acts 2:41).

3. BAPTISM IN THE HOLY SPIRIT

Of the three baptisms, I suspect this third one may be the one that is most misunderstood or confusing for people. But all three are clearly mentioned in Scripture— baptism of salvation, baptism by water, and baptism in the Holy Spirit. Notice the way each one is mentioned in this scene describing the way the disciples preached the Gospel: "Philip went down to a city in Samaria and proclaimed the Messiah there. . . . But when they *believed* Philip as he proclaimed the good news of the kingdom of God and the name of Jesus Christ, they were *baptized*, both men and women" (8:5, 12, my emphasis).

First, the people listening to Philip believed, and then they were baptized with water. But this wasn't the end of the story, because next we're told, "When the apostles in Jerusalem heard that Samaria had accepted the word of God, they sent Peter and John to Samaria. When they arrived, they prayed for the new believers there that they might receive the Holy Spirit, because *the Holy Spirit had not yet come on any of them*; they had simply been baptized in the name of the Lord Jesus. Then Peter and John placed their hands on them, and *they received the Holy Spirit*" (vv. 14–17, my emphasis).

Each of these experiences serves a different purpose. The baptism of salvation confirms that our sins have been forgiven and that our home is in heaven. Water baptism is a public declaration of our new identity as children of God and followers of Jesus. And baptism in the Holy Spirit provides us with spiritual power to minister to and serve others here on earth.

These three experiences reflect the very nature of the Trinity: "For there are three that bear witness in heaven: the Father, the Word, and the Holy Spirit; and these three are one" (1 John 5:7 NKJV). Not convinced? Then consider the verse following this one: "And there are three that bear witness on earth: the Spirit, the water, and the blood; and these three agree as one" (v. 8 NKJV).

Even in the Old Testament we find an example of these three distinct experiences. Before you entered the Holy of Holies in the tabernacle, you encountered three stations: an altar, symbolizing the blood of the Lamb; a laver, representing the cleansing of water; and an oil lamp or candlestick, displaying the power and presence of God's Spirit. These three baptisms reflect our essential relationship with the Holy Spirit. It is through his power that we grow in our faith and live in the freedom we received when we invited Jesus into our life.

While we have the Holy Spirit in our lives with the first two baptisms, we're missing out on an exciting, powerful part of the Christian life if we don't go deeper by experiencing this third baptism in the Spirit. He empowers us to live this life as effectively as possible. God has designed us to live a Spirit-fueled life. To fulfill the Great Commission, the charge Christ gave his followers to share the good news of the gospel with the world, we need the Holy Spirit.

With the Spirit dwelling in us, we have supernatural power. We become bold in our witness to others and can perform signs and wonders to demonstrate God's power. We experience freedom from the power of sin over our lives, as well as freedom to worship with our whole being. The Holy Spirit also helps us maximize prayer, often through a heavenly language, as we express our heart's cry.

EMPOWERED AND EFFECTIVE

Sounds great, right? So how do we practically go about experiencing baptism in the Spirit? Scripture instructs us, "Do not get drunk on wine, which leads to debauchery. Instead, be filled with the Spirit" (Ephesians 5:18). We are called to rely on the Spirit to fill us, but what does this mean? How do we allow him to fill us? Let me suggest four practical ways.

1. REMOVE ALL BARRIERS.

First, do everything in your power to eliminate all obstacles. Pray and confess your sins. Ask God to reveal and remove anything that stands in the way of the Spirit working in your life. Let go of any doctrinal or theological hang-ups—save those for personal study time, consultation with experts, or conversations with other believers—and put aside your pride.

Don't let your mind get in the way of your heart. Don't trust your feelings more than God's Word. God has promised us the gift of his Spirit if we're willing to trust him: "Peter replied, 'Repent and be baptized, every one of you, in the name of Jesus Christ for the forgiveness of your sins. And you will receive the gift of the Holy Spirit. The promise is for you and your children and for all who are far off—for all whom the Lord our God will call'" (Acts 2:38–39).

2. REQUEST THE GIFT OF THE HOLY SPIRIT.

Jesus said that all we have to do is ask, and we will receive the free gift of his presence: "If you then, though you are evil, know how to give good gifts to your children, how much more will your Father in heaven give the Holy Spirit to those who ask him!" (Luke 11:13). I'd say the Holy Spirit is the best gift anyone could ever hope to receive!

Acknowledging and opening this gift is the logical way to proceed. Tell the Lord you want to be baptized in the Holy Spirit. Let him know you want all the gifts associated with the Holy Spirit. You can trust that anything God has for you is good!

3. RECEIVE THE HOLY SPIRIT BY FAITH.

What does it mean to receive the Holy Spirit by faith? And why does it take faith? To put it simply, God is trying to give us things beyond this earthly, mortal realm—supernatural gifts of power, insight, and provision. These gifts may seem like foolishness to our natural, human minds, but we must remember that God's ways are not our ways. His ways may not fit into our logical, sequential, orderly view of how life works.

Most of us would prefer to live in control of our lives—or at least with the illusion that such control is possible. Therefore, our natural minds may fight our attempts to receive the Spirit by faith and to walk by faith daily. This means we have to take some risks and step out of our comfort zones. We must trust God for more than we're capable of doing for ourselves. I don't know about you, but I don't want to stop short of a divine encounter having become satisfied with what I already know!

Stop living life in safe, measured, predictable ways, and allow the Spirit to guide you by faith into uncharted territory. Be careful, though, because the Holy Spirit will gladly take you out of your comfort zone. You might feel prompted to talk to someone about your faith. Or to pay for a meal for someone the Spirit directs you to notice when your family dines out. Or to volunteer to teach a class or lead a Bible study at church. And that's just scratching the surface! Because we're told, "Without faith it is impossible to please God, because anyone who comes to him must believe that he exists and that he rewards those who earnestly seek him" (Hebrews 11:6).

4. RELATE TO HIM DAILY.

Finally, try to relate to the Holy Spirit daily—not in some spooky, weird way, but just as you would with your best friend. Many people relate to God as their heavenly Father and to Jesus as their Savior, their Master, their Lord. The Holy Spirit reflects all these dimensions and more, and seals us as God's children. The Spirit is the breath of fresh air that fills our sails on our spiritual journey.

Talk to the Holy Spirit, and trust that he hears you and is speaking to you as well. Spend time in God's Word, and meditate on what he's saying. Think about how his message applies to your life right now.

Don't be afraid or freaked out about having the Holy Spirit within you. If you're growing in your faith, you probably already have a relationship with Jesus. You're also likely aware of your relationship with God as your Father. But you need an intimate ally, a daily friendship with the Holy Spirit. In fact, here's my prayer for you: "The amazing grace of the Master, Jesus Christ, the extravagant love of God, the intimate friendship of the Holy Spirit, be with all of you" (2 Corinthians 13:14 THE MESSAGE).

YOUR NEXT STEP ON
THE JOURNEY

If you want to develop a stronger faith and a closer relationship with God, then it's time to fully utilize the Holy Spirit's power in your life. What good is a gift if you haven't opened it and started using it? Allow God to bless you with the fullness of all he wants to give you through his Spirit.

This growth process basically occurs in two distinct

ways. First, allow the Holy Spirit to show you areas of your life that need to change. Scripture warns us, "Don't grieve God. Don't break his heart. His Holy Spirit, moving and breathing in you, is the most intimate part of your life, making you fit for himself. Don't take such a gift for granted" (Ephesians 4:30 THE MESSAGE). To effect change in our lives, either we use external constraints—something outside ourselves telling us how to behave and controlling our attitudes, opinions, and actions—or we rely on internal change, something inside us directing us in the way we should behave. Only God's Spirit can fuel this internal change in us: "I will give you a new heart and put a new spirit in you; I will remove from you your heart of stone and give you a heart of flesh. And I will put my Spirit in you and move you to follow my decrees and be careful to keep my laws" (Ezekiel 36:26–27).

You can't change what you can't see, but the Holy Spirit sees everything! Ask him to put his finger on any area that's not right in your life. Let him point out areas where God is not pleased. Pray this prayer: "Search me, God, and know my heart; test me and know my anxious thoughts. See if there is any offensive way in me, and lead me in the way everlasting" (Psalm 139:23–24). Then do what it takes to eliminate that sin and draw closer to him. He will show you what needs to change and will lead you in the everlasting way.

Another Spirit-fueled way of growing in your faith is letting the Holy Spirit change you rather than trying so hard to change yourself. This may sound counterintuitive to what we just considered, but it's actually complementary. Yes, when the Holy Spirit reveals an area in which we need to change, we are wise to heed him. Yet at the same time, we don't have to rely on our own power to grow spiritually.

So many people are exhausted from trying to be a better person. They do everything in their own strength. Instead, invite the Holy Spirit to do a work on the inside. Let him make you an entirely brand-new person. As Paul wrote to the church in Corinth, "For the Lord is the Spirit, and wherever the Spirit of the Lord is, there is freedom. . . . And the Lord—who is the Spirit—makes us more and more like him as we are changed into his glorious image" (2 Corinthians 3:17–18 NLT).

One of the primary functions of the Holy Spirit is to put a holy spirit in you! Being filled with the Holy Spirit doesn't make me better than you; it makes me better than *me*. If you want real, lasting change, then turn the Holy Spirit loose in your life and watch what happens.

SECTION 3

DISCOVER PURPOSE

What motivates you to get out of bed in the morning? Do you know why you do what you do? How often do you feel like you were made for more?

I suspect many of us feel frustrated and discontent with our lives because we're not living out the specific, unique purpose God has given us. We know there has to be more than the life we're experiencing, but we don't know how to access it. Such frustration reminds me of a story I once heard about a greyhound racetrack in Florida. If you've never seen one of these races, these big beautiful dogs line up to sprint after a mechanical rabbit leading them around the track. In this particular race, just as the dogs were released, the bunny 'bot exploded! With the rabbit gone, the pursuing greyhounds didn't know what to do.

One immediately sat down and rested. Another became so confused he dashed through the fence and hurt himself. Several dogs howled and barked at the spectators in the stands. But not one single dog finished the race—because there was nothing to chase!

This incident strikes me as a vivid picture of the way many people live. When there's nothing to chase, they struggle to find meaning in their lives. They sit down and get stuck where they are, try various escape routes only to hurt themselves, howl (and tweet) at others, and eventually give up the race.

But it's not just having a rabbit to chase. The key to a significant life is making sure you're chasing something much bigger than what's right in front of you. So many people work to achieve career goals and amass wealth, only to end up disappointed and disillusioned by their success. Others think finding the right spouse, starting a family, or serving in ministry will fulfill them, only to experience exhaustion instead of exhilaration. They catch their rabbits only to be disappointed.

That's why it's so important to know why you're chasing what you're chasing. You need a clear focus on what matters most to fuel your motivations. You need a sense of purpose bigger than just more money, a nicer house, or the recognition of others.

The good news is that God has a unique and distinct purpose for your life. He has designed you specifically for the calling he has put on your life. Our loving Creator invites each of us to experience the joyous adventure of fulfilling the potential he has placed inside us.

You already have what it takes.

You just have to unlock it!

GRACE HAS BEEN GIVEN

Every person wonders about their purpose at different points in their life. Regrettably, many people never discover a direction that draws on all their gifts, talents, abilities, and passions. They flounder from place to place, relationship to relationship, job to job, always knowing there has to be more but not knowing how to tap into it.

Nonbelievers as well as those who have committed to following Christ experience this aimlessness. In fact, I estimate that nine out of ten people who know God do *not* know their God-given purpose. This gap in the church is even more striking when we realize that God not only wants us to know our own individual purpose, but he also wants us to help others know their unique purpose:

> But to each one of us grace has been given as Christ apportioned it. . . . So Christ himself gave the apostles, the prophets, the evangelists, the pastors and teachers, to equip his people for works of service, so that the body of Christ may be built up until we all reach unity in the faith and in the knowledge of the Son of God and become mature, attaining to the whole measure of the fullness of Christ. (Ephesians 4:7, 11–13)

In the first sentence, the word translated *grace* means a special gift, a divine enablement. It's not a reference to grace as we think of it in relation to God's mercy and our salvation. Instead, this kind of grace refers to something you do that brings fulfillment and makes a difference in the lives of those around you. We see a reference to this same kind of grace in Paul's letter to the Christians in

Rome: "We have different *gifts*, according to the *grace* given to each of us" (Romans 12:6, my emphasis).

Our enemy, however, tries to confuse our identities. The last thing he wants is for us to operate out of our God-given purpose at full throttle. A major part of his plan revolves around preventing us from knowing and living out our purpose. No matter how he tries, though, the devil cannot keep us from using the gifts God has placed within us. We simply have to unlock them and actualize them through the power of the Holy Spirit.

We're told, "For *you created my inmost being*; you knit me together in my mother's womb. I praise you because I am fearfully and wonderfully made; your works are wonderful, *I know that full well*. . . . All the days ordained for me were written in your book before one of them came to be" (Psalm 139:13, 14, 16, my emphasis). If you look closely at how God has made you, then you will discover what your life is all about. It's already there inside you.

LIVING ON PURPOSE

As we shift into this third section on spiritual growth, Discover Purpose, my prayer for you is the same Paul prayed for believers, to know the hope of your calling: "I pray that the eyes of your heart may be enlightened in order that you may know the hope to which he has called you, the riches of his glorious inheritance in his holy people" (Ephesians 1:18).

Don't miss the way hope and calling are connected. Basically, you'll never have hope for a better, richer, more fulfilled life until you know what God has called you to do with your life. Nothing else will satisfy you or utilize all he has placed within you the same way. Once you know your sacred purpose, you experience hope more fully.

Seeing someone live out their calling with purpose and passion is incredibly inspiring. We all want that sense of significance found in achieving something bigger than just monetary or material success. Because we're eternal, spiritual beings, we yearn to create an eternal, spiritual legacy.

We see this yearning played out in Paul's life. His whole life was wrapped around his purpose. He wrote, "I consider my life worth nothing to me; my only aim is to finish the race and complete the task the Lord Jesus has given me" (Acts 20:24).

Knowing your purpose is second only to knowing Christ as your Savior. When you know what you're made for, you can take your eyes off yourself and focus on serving others as God has wired you to do. In other words, your problems seem smaller when your purpose is bigger! Paul explained how purpose provides a wellspring of hope and joy:

Therefore we do not lose heart. Though outwardly we are wasting away, yet inwardly we are being renewed day by day. For our light and momentary troubles are achieving for us an eternal glory that far outweighs them all. So we fix our eyes not on what is seen, but on what is unseen, since what is seen is temporary, but what is unseen is eternal. (2 Corinthians 4:16–18)

Paul certainly had his share of problems—violent mobs, trouble with Jewish leaders and the Roman government, shipwrecks, jail time, just to name a few—but they didn't have the same effect as they would have had on others. Why? Because Paul wasn't focused on them. He had something bigger in his life that he was focused on: his God-given purpose.

I'm convinced that the secret to solving our problems isn't to solve them. Even if we solve one problem, another is sure to take its place. The real secret to solving problems is to have something bigger in your life, something greater and more meaningful than any earthly problem. You're welcome to keep trying to solve your problems your way. But the real solution is found in God's way.

True happiness is found in purpose.

CHAPTER SEVEN

SPIRITUAL GIFTS

YOU WERE MADE FOR THIS

I meet many people who have learned more about themselves by studying their genealogy with DNA testing. You've probably seen the ads for popular companies like Ancestry.com and 23andMe that offer DNA-testing kits. You pay the fee, receive your kit, and send back a saliva sample, which is then analyzed to reveal your ethnic and cultural origins.

These tests usually confirm what people already know, such as that their ancestors came from Western Europe or Africa or Asia, but sometimes they discover something that surprises them. Maybe a percentage of their genetic makeup reveals ancestors from South America or the Middle East. Knowing their ethnic and cultural heritage helps many people understand, accept, and celebrate certain aspects of their family, their identity, and their unique personality.

Whether we know the details of our DNA or not, we're all called to embrace who God made us to be. This acceptance was certainly one of the keys to King David's success. He knew who he was, embraced it, and celebrated it. He wrote, "I thank you, High God—you're breathtaking! Body and soul, I am marvelously made! I worship in adoration—what a creation!" (Psalm 139:14 THE MESSAGE).

Maybe you think David's poetic words sound arrogant, but I disagree. David was simply sure of who he was because he knew *whose* he was. David accepted the marvel of who he was not because of anything he had done or could do, but because he knew God's creative power and artistry. David continued:

> You know me inside and out, you know every bone in my body; You know exactly how I was made, bit by bit, how I was sculpted from nothing into something. Like an open book, you watched me grow from conception to birth; all the stages of my life were spread out before you, the days of my life all prepared before I'd even lived one day. (vv. 15–16 THE MESSAGE)

Although he was God's anointed king of Israel, David was no better than you and me. We, too, have been "marvelously made" by our Creator, fashioned in his own image to reflect his glory. We're told, "For we are God's handiwork, created in Christ Jesus to do good works, which God prepared in advance for us to do" (Ephesians 2:10). Notice that God creates us and prepares us to do good works before we actually do them. He has a purpose in mind for each of us before we are born.

This makes sense if we consider the way we often create solutions and invent new products and devices. You have something you want to accomplish—a need, a purpose—so you create something to fulfill that need and accomplish the purpose. You decide what you want your new creation to do, and then you design it and build it accordingly.

For instance, if you wanted to make a drinking container for people to take with them wherever they go, you would want it to be light and portable. It would need to be hollow, of course, and able to stand upright on its own with an opening to fit a person's mouth. Knowing your creation's purpose allows you to design it according to that purpose. Similarly, if you look at how something is made, you find clues to its purpose. People could probably tell your water bottle was designed to hold liquid without being told.

We reflect the same kind of engineering—only on a divine scale. Before time began God knew something he wanted each of us to do. Then he designed us specifically for that purpose. Your divine design illuminates the destiny God has for you. If you discover the way you have been made, it will point to what God wants you to do with your life.

Design reveals destiny.

DISCOVER YOUR DESIGN

So how do you begin to discover your design? There are as many different tests, assessments, indicators, and personality systems as there are individual people—well, maybe not that many, but close! At our church we take people through several different assessments to help them discover their God-given design. Often, various tests and instruments need to be taken at different points in your life to reflect a clear pattern of your strengths, talents, gifts, and abilities.

The DISC profile of assessing personality is often a good, basic place to begin. It's loosely based on the four classical temperaments and reveals patterns of behavior tied to your personality. Here's a brief overview of the four types:

D: Choleric—Dominance, Directness (task oriented, decisive, organized, outgoing, outspoken)

I: Sanguine—Influence, Interest in people (witty, easygoing, outgoing, people oriented)

S: Phlegmatic—Steadiness, Stability (analytical, people oriented, introverted)

C: Melancholy—Compliance, Competence (task oriented, goal oriented, introverted)

You might have taken a DISC test in the past, or the Myers-Briggs or StrengthsFinder assessments. Again, I recommend using a variety of tools instead of relying on just one. I would also caution you against self-identifying or assuming you already know all there is to know about yourself. Take the tests, reflect on the results, and discuss your thoughts with other believers you trust. These personality assessments are a helpful place to start as you seek a deeper understanding of the way you were made and the purpose to which your various traits might be pointing. But don't stop there.

Your purpose can also be found in one or more of the following three areas.

1. YOUR GIFTS AND PASSIONS

We have different gifts, according to the grace given to each of us. If your gift is prophesying, then prophesy in accordance with your faith; if it is serving, then serve; if it is teaching, then teach; if it is to encourage, then give encouragement; if it is giving, then give generously; if it is to lead, do it diligently; if it is to show mercy, do it cheerfully. (Romans 12:6–8)

Your gifts and passions are the areas you love and naturally excel in. Sometimes they are easy to spot, but not always. You may need to pursue various topics, issues, and abilities to filter through the possibilities and discover the ones you find most compelling. As we see in the above passage, our gifts emerge from the grace we've each been given, and we're clearly intended to use them for the good of others.

2. YOUR LIFE EXPERIENCE

> So here's what I want you to do, God helping you: Take your everyday, ordinary life—your sleeping, eating, going-to-work, and walking-around life—and place it before God as an offering. Embracing what God does for you is the best thing you can do for him. (Romans 12:1 THE MESSAGE)

God will often use you in the events and situations you experience. As this verse points out, even moments that seem mundane and ordinary can be used by God to fulfill his purposes—in your life and in the lives of those around you. We may assume that if we're not up front on Sunday mornings or called to some exotic mission field, then our experience doesn't count for the kingdom. But if we're willing to serve, God uses us everywhere in every way, day in and day out.

3. YOUR PAIN

> All praise to God, the Father of our Lord Jesus Christ. God is our merciful Father and the source of all comfort. He comforts us in all our troubles so that we can comfort others. When they are troubled, we will be

able to give them the same comfort God has given us. (2 Corinthians 1:3–4 NLT)

As uncomfortable as it may be, this verse reminds us that God even uses our wounds and struggles. That means we need to learn to value the bad days and hard times too. If you've ever been comforted by someone who understood what you were going through, then you know how powerful this understanding can be. God will often use us to help others in the place where we've felt pain—if we'll let him.

MADE TO MINISTER

No matter what your unique personality design reveals itself to be, no matter what you discover your divine purpose to be, we are all called to reflect God's character. This means you should yourself be a minister as much as anyone on staff at your church is. Now, obviously I'm not talking about the profession or vocation of being a pastor or minister. I'm talking about someone who brings the ministry of Jesus to others. We're told, "But you are a chosen people, a royal priesthood, a holy nation, God's special possession, that you may declare the praises of him who called you out of darkness into his wonderful light" (1 Peter 2:9).

Notice here that if you know God, then you're responsible for sharing what he has done in your life. You have the same direct access to God and the power of the

Holy Spirit that I do—or anyone else who knows him. Sometimes people think that pastors have special connections they don't have the same access to. I see this when I play golf and the weather turns, and one of my buddies will say, "You're a pastor—do something!" I always tell them, "I'm in sales—not management!"

We are all on an equal playing field before God, called to reflect him to the world, whether we're professional ministers or not. I don't have any special connections as a pastor. There's not an A-list and a B-list of those who serve God and his people. Some people say, "Chris, you have the most important gift, because you're the preacher!" But that's simply not true. Every role is important. I'm just using my gifts as God has called me to do. And he calls you to do the same with the gifts he has given you.

There's no such thing as a small player in God's eyes. We're all teammates. Everybody is needed—which means if you don't contribute, we all suffer. Every task is vital to the work to further God's kingdom. The Bible reminds us, "All of you together are Christ's body, and each of you is a part of it" (1 Corinthians 12:27 NLT).

ONE OF A KIND

We are all wired differently by God for a deliberate purpose. Each one is unique. You're not one in a million—or even a billion. You're one of a kind.

Some people think they have nothing to contribute. They have believed the enemy's lies that they're not talented, capable, or smart enough to serve God. The devil doesn't want you owning the truth of who you are and serving out of it. He wants to disable you and take you out.

The truth is that God has given each of us special gifts. He is the ultimate Creator, and he designed us to fulfill the abilities he planted inside us. Even when we share common gifts and goals with other people, we discover that each of us is needed. Each of us has something personal and distinct to offer. We're reminded of this truth in God's Word:

> God's various gifts are handed out everywhere; but they all originate in God's Spirit. God's various ministries are carried out everywhere; but they all originate in God's Spirit. God's various expressions of power are in action everywhere; but God himself is behind it all. Each person is given something to do that shows who God is: Everyone gets in on it, everyone benefits. All kinds of things are handed out by the Spirit, and to all kinds of people! The variety is wonderful.
> (1 Corinthians 12:4–7 THE MESSAGE)

I love that last line—variety is wonderful! God makes every one of us unique, so he must love variety. Just as no two snowflakes or fingerprints are the same, neither are our unique abilities from God. When you discover the way he made you and begin living out of it, you'll experience a fulfillment unlike any other. You will know, *I was made for this!*

No matter where you are on your journey of faith, no matter what you've done in the past or how you might have messed up, no matter how average or untalented you think you are, you are special and have a special gift. God wants to use you—all of you.

I've had a recurring dream for years. I dream of a church where every person knows who God called them to be. In the church I grew up in, Sunday night services were more informal. Sometimes our pastor would deem it "testimony night" and pass the microphone around and let people tell how God had answered prayer or provided for them that week. Those testimonies were spontaneous and unfiltered, sometimes funny but always heartfelt.

So I dream of passing the mic around and letting people share how they're living out God's purpose for their lives. It might sound something like this:

"My name is John, and I'm a Christian with the spiritual gift of mercy. I serve at the Dream Center, because I love helping those who are helpless—the homeless, the runaways, the addicts. I was made for this!"

"Hey, I'm Lynn! I'm a follower of Jesus Christ with the spiritual gift of administration. I serve in Highlands kids' church where I make sure kids get securely checked in and picked up by their parents or another designated member of our church family. I love it when the system works. I was made for this!"

"Hello, I'm Mary. God created me to serve and gave me the gift of helping, so I stuff worship guides. I feel like I'm responsible to get the word out there. I was made for this!"

"Hi, everyone. I'm Courtney. I'm sixteen, and God saved me. I'm just so grateful. I lead a small group of friends at my high school in a little Bible study. I guess I have the gift of evangelism. I was made for this!"

"I'm Mike, and I'm a priest—well, not a literal one! But I have the spiritual gift of leadership. I lead a small group at my home and love serving others in this way. I was made for this!"

"Hey, y'all. I'm Ashley. I love Jesus, and I have the spiritual gift of encouragement. My small group goes to nursing homes just to talk to and visit with the residents there. Those people are so dear to me! I leave thinking, *I was made for this!*"

"I really love to pray—my name's Martha—so I think I have the spiritual gift of intercession. My kids are all grown now, so I have a lot of time on my hands. A lot of days I just stay home and pray for everyone I know and the needs they have. I believe I'm making a difference, because I was made for this!"

"Howdy! I'm Matt, and my spiritual gift must be being goofy! I love to laugh, so I just hang out with the junior high kids. I love making them feel special and helping them realize how much God loves them. Don't laugh, but I was made for this!"

Now it's *your* turn. What would you say?

YOUR NEXT STEP ON THE JOURNEY

We'd all like to change something about ourselves. But God accepts us exactly as we are. He doesn't want to change us; he wants to redeem us.

If you'll let him, God will show you how you can be used by him in a great way. Once you discover your portion, that special purpose for which he designed you, then you will experience a joy, peace, and fulfillment like no other. When you love your assignment in life, you love your life.

The following short exercise is designed to help you think about what you already know about yourself and your purpose and what you still wish you knew. Spend a few moments in prayer before you begin, then complete the following:

If you had to sum up what you believe your God-given purpose to be, you would say:

_____

_____

_____

The evidence for this conclusion would include:

_____

_____

_____

If you're not aware of your purpose yet, what's one step you can take to help you discover it? Perhaps you could meet with another Christian, someone who knows you well and whom you trust, and ask them the following questions:

1. What gifts and abilities do you believe God has placed in me?
2. How would you describe who I am and my purpose to someone who doesn't know me?
3. What's a next step you recommend to help me discover more about my purpose and the way God has made me?

CHAPTER EIGHT

THE BODY OF CHRIST

YOU CAN'T BE YOU
WITHOUT ME

I dated a lot before getting married. It's not something I'm proud of, and I don't think it was necessarily good or bad. It was just my experience as a young adult at the time. I knew I wanted to be married someday, so I figured I had to start somewhere, and dating seemed like the natural place to begin. Those relationships were fun and for the most part healthy, but I didn't receive the fullness of what I was ultimately looking for—a wife—because those relationships lacked something foundational to marriage—commitment.

When I met and later proposed to Tammy, we moved our relationship from dating to marriage. I stood at the altar and committed myself to her. We made vows to each other before God. With those wedding vows, we anticipated experiencing both the full benefits and inherent responsibilities of our lifetime commitment.

Once our commitment was in place, we could then enjoy a level of intimacy reserved exclusively for husband and wife. We became responsible for one another, in sickness and in health, for richer or poorer, in good times and in hard times. We no longer dated or looked for intimacy in any other relationships. We had each other and made a commitment that included all areas of our lives.

Maybe it's because we're told that marriage illustrates the way Christ loves the church (Ephesians 5:22–32), but I believe God wants each of us to commit to a local church the same way a couple commits to one another in marriage. God wants us doing more than just dating and enjoying ourselves as we jump from church to church. He wants us to be committed and contributing, a member and not merely an attender.

A commitment certainly requires more from you, but it also provides opportunities for intimacy that wouldn't exist otherwise. In other words, membership has its privileges!

CALLED TO COMMIT

At Church of the Highlands we recognize the need for each person who takes part in our community to have a formal membership, a committed relationship to our church family. We ask people to commit to membership for four reasons that reflect the biblical, cultural, practical, and personal basis for such a commitment. The first reason is clear enough. Jesus is committed to the church: "Christ loved the church and gave himself up for her" (Ephesians 5:25). The church is described in the Bible as the bride of Christ, his beloved (vv. 22–32). Again, this picture reflects the commitment and intimacy we experience with God not only individually but also corporately, as one body of believers.

The cultural reason for committing to a church emerges from the way the church provides an antidote to the commitment phobia of our society and popular culture. God's Word makes it clear that as followers of Christ we are set apart from the world and its ways: "For you are a people holy to the LORD your God. Out of all the peoples on the face of the earth, the LORD has chosen you to be his treasured possession" (Deuteronomy 14:2). We're called to be in the world but not of it (John 17:15–17). And this is difficult to do without the support and accountability of a committed community of believers.

We live in an age when very few people are willing to be committed to anything: a job, a marriage, our country. This cultural attitude has produced a mindset of "church shoppers and hoppers." If you don't like the worship music, go somewhere else. If the preacher's sermon offended you, find a church with a pastor you like. If you don't like the décor of the sanctuary, find one that suits your taste. I wish I were exaggerating, but sadly I'm not.

Membership swims against the current of our culture's "consumer religion." Committing to your local church is an unselfish decision. It forces you to stick with this community of believers through good times and bad, through joyful seasons and painful storms, in sickness and in health. Commitment always builds character.

The third reason is quite practical. Committed membership in a church defines who can be counted on—to serve, to give, to contribute, to support, to grow, to love, to forgive, and to celebrate. Every functional, healthy organization relies on knowing specifically upon whom it can rely. Every team has a roster. Every school has an enrollment. Every business has a payroll. Every army has an enlistment. Even our country takes a census and requires voter registration.

Membership identifies our family—where we belong.

Finally, there's a personal reason you should commit to the church: it cultivates and nurtures your spiritual growth. The New Testament places a major emphasis on the need for Christians to be accountable to each other for spiritual growth. James 5:16 instructs, "Therefore confess your sins to each other and pray for each other so that you may be healed. The prayer of a righteous person is powerful and effective." You cannot be accountable when you're not committed to any specific church family. Accountability helps our faith mature. It spurs us toward growth, so we don't want to miss out on this unique benefit afforded by our Christian family.

Active participation in your local church provides opportunities to hear, learn, study, and grow in God's Word. Individual Bible study is good and important but has certain limitations. When you're in a community dedicated to studying the Word together, you gain insight you might not have discovered on your own into the various layers and dimensions of God's Word, along with its application and relevancy to your life. You also have opportunities to share your gifts with others, whether through teaching, hospitality, administration, intercession, or whatever yours may be.

As you consider these four reasons—biblical, cultural, practical, and personal—for investing deeply in church community, you'll find that community provides pillars of support for you in all areas of your life. And by God's design, it will also lead you to finding or fulfilling your purpose, something you can't do without a church family. Why? Because we're all connected to one another. God designed us in his own image as relational beings. We're a body, a flock, a fellowship.

Your purpose cannot exist in a vacuum. Your gifts are designed to be used to serve and to meet the needs of the rest of the body. What good is it if you find out what part of the body you are but don't use it? You're only as successful as you are when you're connected to other people in your church community.

Forgive me for a quick but gross illustration: If you cut off someone's hand, that person's body will continue to grow. But, of course, the severed hand will not grow. It will shrivel and die. For that hand to grow, it must be connected to the body it's part of. If you're a believer and not connected with a body of believers, then you, too, will shrivel and diminish. You'll feel just as awful as that severed hand!

God's Word is clear: "The whole body, supported and held together by its ligaments and sinews, grows as God causes it to grow" (Colossians 2:19). I can't be me without you. You can't be you without me—and the others around you.

Let me leave you with one final picture of the way we are meant to commit and relate to the church. Years ago, my family and I lived in Colorado. While I loved living there for many reasons, I especially liked the groves of aspen trees growing along the hillsides and mountain slopes. Not only do they shimmer beautifully when the wind blows through thousands of their small, spade-shaped leaves, but aspen trees always grow in groups. In fact, their roots become intertwined so that they all share the same nutrients. The health and growth of one aspen depends on the other related trees around it.

Your health and growth depend on the people around you.

Their health and growth depend on *you*.

YOUR NEXT STEP ON
THE JOURNEY

The Bible uses the word *church* in two different ways. First, it's used to refer to every Christian who has ever lived throughout history. This is called the historical, universal church. Every believer all around the world—regardless of their denominational label, regardless of whether they meet with other believers in a church building or outside, in a tent or a little hut, or wherever they may be during whatever era they live—is part of the universal church.

The second way *church* is used is to refer to a local group, a specific place. For example, think of the church at Corinth, the church that met in Lydia's home, the church that was on the hill, or the church in your city. In this context, *church* is used in a concrete, specific, local sense.

Consider that the Bible uses the general, universal term only four times. Which means that almost every time you see the word *church* in your Bible, it's used to refer to a specific group of believers like your own church today.

Once you became a believer, you automatically became a part of the historical, universal church of God. It happened immediately the moment you gave your life to Christ. You didn't have to apply or fill out any forms. You're in!

But you don't become a part of a local church until you make a deliberate commitment. Like the decision to stop dating and commit to one person in marriage, you're called to find your church home and make a long-term commitment. Maybe you're already part of a community of believers and have made this kind of commitment. Or maybe you're part of one but need to take the next step and commit wholeheartedly. Or you might be just starting the process of looking for a church home, one where you know you belong. While there's no set number of churches you should visit before you decide, I encourage you to pray and ask the Holy Spirit to guide you. Generally, here's how the process often unfolds:

1. **Visit some local churches in your area.** Ask friends and family where they belong, and see if they're willing for you to visit with them. Look online at church websites, and watch a service or sermon to get a feel for what each one is like. Make a list of churches that seem to resonate with your beliefs, needs, and longings.

2. **Get information about the church, and/or attend the membership class.** After you've visited and believe you're ready to move toward committing, learn all you can about the church, its leaders, other members, its various ministries, and the core beliefs. Make sure it's a Bible-based church that clearly preaches the gospel of salvation through Jesus Christ. Talk to members who have long been a part of your new prospective church. Ask them what they love about their church, as well as what they might want to change.

3. **Listen carefully for the vision of the church.** Where is this church going? What do its members believe God is calling them to do? What does this church need to fulfill its vision? How does the church's vision align with what you believe God is calling you to do? Vision compatibility is often the most important indicator that a church will be a good home for you.

4. **Listen to the Holy Spirit.** Again, stay in close communication with God's Spirit and pay attention to how he speaks to you. The church is a family, a spiritual family of brothers and sisters. God will lead you. Let him.

We are the body of Christ. And just like the parts of your body can't be what they are meant to be without the rest of the body, neither can you be who you are meant to be without the other members of the church. None of us can be who we are meant to be without being connected to other believers.

Commit to your church, and be all you can be!

CHAPTER NINE

GROWTH

THE MOST EXCITING PART
OF CHRISTIANITY

Every year I take time between Christmas and the New Year to pray, to review the recent past, and to dream about the near future. As part of this process, I ask God for a word, a focal point for my life for the coming twelve months. Most recently, as I began this year, God gave me a surprising word: *grow*. Surprising because you would think, after forty years of being a Christian and thirty-five years in ministry, I wouldn't need to focus on growth. The more I considered it, though, the more it humbled and encouraged me. Because the truth is there's always room to grow!

I sat down and wrote out areas where I wanted to grow. I thought about ways I wanted to grow as a husband, a father, a friend, and a man of God. I reflected on how I wanted to be a catalyst for my family to grow—not literally, though, unless it's more grandkids!

Then I started thinking about the church I lead and how I wanted it to grow. Instead of looking back over the year and feeling satisfied because we had a great year, I became excited to press on for more. This wasn't a sense of being driven to achieve more but rather a genuine exhilaration at knowing God had more for us.

In a few short weeks, I noticed that a new energy came into my prayer life. I became more focused on the gift of the present moment and how I could serve that day. As the weeks turned into months, I saw clearly just how much I needed God to nudge me toward new growth. And I remain excited to see what he has in store for me next!

GROWING TOGETHER

You don't have to wait on God to give you a signal in order to pursue spiritual growth. He wants us all to grow. In fact, it's a biblical mandate:

So Christ himself gave the apostles, the prophets, the evangelists, the pastors and teachers, to equip his people for works of service, so that the body of Christ may be *built up* until we all reach unity in the faith and in the knowledge of the Son of God and *become mature*, attaining to the whole measure of the fullness of Christ.

Then we will no longer be infants, tossed back and forth by the waves, and blown here and there by every wind of teaching and by the cunning and craftiness of people in their deceitful scheming. Instead, speaking the truth in love, *we will grow* to become in every respect the mature body of him who is the head, that is, Christ. From him the whole body, joined and held together by every supporting ligament, *grows* and builds itself up in love, as each part does its work. (Ephesians 4:11–16, my emphasis)

As we go about doing the work to which God calls each of us, we naturally grow. We grow closer to him. We grow to rely on him more. We grow stronger in our faith and our willingness to trust him—even when life is painful and we can't tell what he's up to. Our growth has no end point in this earthly life—there's always more to learn, to observe, to discover, to enjoy.

Steady spiritual growth keeps us focused and anchored amid life's many storms. We don't have to be blown and tossed around by the winds and waves of changing circumstances. Our faith in God is our foundation. He is our solid rock that never moves. We're told, "Every good and perfect gift is from above, coming down from the

Father of the heavenly lights, who does not change like shifting shadows" (James 1:17).

Moreover, our growth is critical to the mission God has given us. We're part of a body. Bodies are living organisms that grow. If one part doesn't grow, the rest can't function well. Echoing what we discussed in the previous chapter, we're all interdependent within the body of Christ. Like the roots of the trees in an aspen grove, when we flourish, everyone else benefits. And when we flounder, others miss out on what we have to offer.

You can't be you without the rest of the body.

They can't be who they're called to be without you.

We're all growing together!

ENJOY THE CLIMB

I shared the word I received from God this past year to emphasize that we're all continually called to grow. In certain seasons, we experience more growth than in others, and that growth is easy to see. But when spiritual growth is less obvious, we may doubt we're making any forward progress. That's when we have to trust that we're growing even if we don't see it or feel it.

It's like when we were kids lying in the grass and trying to watch the flowers grow. When growth is all we're focused on, we may not notice the slow, gradual ways it sometimes happens. If we're devoted to becoming more like Jesus each day, allowing the Holy Spirit to guide and direct us, then we're definitely growing in our faith.

One of the only ways not to grow is to settle. Pursuing growth keeps us from settling for less than God's best for our lives. Sometimes I think it's human nature to settle and stay put. And I'm not talking about a season of rest or a Sabbath period—I'm talking about resigning ourselves to what we already have and giving up. As tempting as it may be to enjoy the security that settling seems to bring, we're called to so much more. We simply can't settle for less when there's so much more to do!

Even though we don't want to settle, we also don't want to miss out on the blessings in front of us because we're overly focused on what's ahead. Healthy spiritual growth strikes a balance between being very content and very dissatisfied at the same time. We're content with what God has for us, all that he has given us, and how he has provided for us. We're grateful for the many ways he works through us to bless others. Yet at the same time we refuse to rest on past success!

If what you did yesterday still looks big to you, you aren't growing today. As the legendary Babe Ruth said, "Yesterday's home runs don't win today's games." I love the example the great evangelist John Wesley gave of another preacher. Every seven years, he would burn all his past sermons! Wesley quotes him as saying, "It is a shame if I cannot write better sermons now than I did seven years ago."[1]

We don't necessarily need to destroy past accomplishments, but growth does require an intentional process. Otherwise, we get so consumed by the daily, the urgent, the temporary that we never make time for the transcendent, the significant, and the eternal. Healthy, consistent growth requires a four-step plan:

1. Set aside time to grow.
2. Determine your specific area of growth.
3. Find resources in this area of growth.
4. Apply what you begin learning.

Following your growth plan should challenge you, and it may get downright hard before you notice any change. Iconic radio broadcaster Paul Harvey used to say, "You can tell you're on the road to success; it's uphill all the way." Remember, though, you're going to have to climb some hills if you want to reach new heights—so enjoy the climb!

CHANGE IS CONSTANT

In addition to requiring a deliberate plan of action, growth involves a willingness to change. If we keep doing everything the same way, it's tough to discover anything new. If we don't change, we don't grow.

Growth demands a surrender of security as we embrace change in pursuit of new discoveries. To grow, we can't refuse to consider what others believe by constantly defending our current positions. Yes, stick to your values and use the Bible to keep God's standards always in front of you, but don't defend why you stay where you are in a particular area. Approach new ideas with an open mind. Trust that God's Spirit will give you discernment and his Word will provide wisdom.

In order to grow, you will likely need to change some habits. You will never change your life until you change something you do daily! You can't grow toward a stronger relationship with your spouse if you don't change the way you usually communicate. You can't improve your financial health if you keep spending the same way on the same items. You can't enjoy more contentment and peace if you aren't willing to adjust your attitude.

As you learn to embrace change and pursue growth, you will find that this process naturally produces joy. Every time I start pursuing growth in a certain area of my life, I experience a ripple effect in all areas. I feel happier and able to enjoy the journey that unfolds with each new day. And my prayer life becomes better because I've given my faith a target!

If you're struggling to enjoy your life and rarely experience much joy, the best spiritual prescription I can offer you is to focus on growth. Identify areas where you want to learn more or improve yourself, change up the way you've been doing things, and see what happens. Don't focus on someone else's growth and joy; focus on your own!

GROW IN WISDOM

Although we have only one verse summarizing the life of Jesus from age twelve to age thirty, it still packs a punch: "And Jesus grew in wisdom and stature, and in favor with God and man" (Luke 2:52). While we don't know specifically how he grew, it's clear he didn't just stand around and wait for it to happen.

Notice that he grew in wisdom. Like most Jewish boys growing up, Jesus studied his culture and faith on a regular basis. Maybe it's easier for children and teens to learn because they're often hungry for knowledge and curious about all that they don't know. In my humble opinion, though, we need to keep this curiosity and desire to learn and grow throughout our entire lives. Too many adults are satisfied with what they already know. They've settled and, in the process, stunted their own growth: "If the ax is dull and its edge unsharpened, more strength is needed, but *skill* will bring *success*" (Ecclesiastes 10:10, my emphasis).

As we assess our growth and spiritual development, too often we focus on the wrong measurement. The most important question to determine growth is not "What am I doing?" but rather "Who am I becoming?" It means a shift from thinking about what is seen to thinking about what is unseen, from what is obvious to what is deeper and wiser.

Wisdom is one of the fruits of growing in our faith. One of the easiest ways to stimulate our own growth toward wisdom is to learn from the wisdom of others. Being curious about people, observing them, respecting their different ways of doing things and their different perspectives—all help you stretch yourself. Teachers, pastors, bosses, friends, and mentors are invaluable resources. Given the opportunity, ask them direct questions to help nourish your personal growth and development. Here are a few, which I've used in one form or another, that you might consider:

1. What is the greatest leadership lesson you've learned?
2. What are you learning now?
3. How has failure shaped your life?
4. Who do you know that I should know?
5. What have you read that I should read?
6. What have you done that I should do?
7. What question should I have asked that I didn't ask?
8. How can I add value to you?

GROW IN STATURE

To return to the verse about Jesus' growth (Luke 2:52), notice that he grew not only in wisdom, but also in stature. He grew taller and stronger, passing from childhood into adolescence into adulthood. But growing physically doesn't happen by accident either. Our bodies require healthy food, clean water, regular exercise, fresh air, and plenty of sleep.

Once we reach adulthood, we may be tempted for a while to ignore our body's needs, especially for proper nutrition and adequate rest. But over time, our bodies remind us of our physical limitations. Our bodies are temporary, and while they're resilient and amazing, they are also fragile. If you want to grow in all areas of your life, then you have to take care of your body.

While it may seem obvious, the best suggestion I can make for keeping your body healthy is to take control of your schedule. Not everything doable is sustainable! Again, we have to learn to discern between what's truly important and what's merely urgent.

Is what we're so frantic about worth our time, energy, and resources? Will it matter a year from now? Five years from now? When I'm thinking about the finite time and energy I have to invest each day, I like to remember that my goal is to build something eternal. My test, based on the following passage from the Bible, is to ask myself whether what I'm focusing on will last:

By the grace God has given me, I laid a foundation as a wise builder, and someone else is building on it. But each one should build with care. For no one can lay any foundation other than the one already laid, which is Jesus Christ. If anyone builds on this foundation using gold, silver, costly stones, wood, hay or straw, their work will be shown for what it is, because the Day will bring it to light. It will be revealed with fire, and the fire will test the quality of each person's work. If what has been built *survives*, the builder will receive a reward. If it is burned up, the builder will suffer loss but yet will be saved—even though only as one escaping through the flames. (1 Corinthians 3:10–15, my emphasis)

Your body can only take so much. God designed us with bodies capable of working hard, but we still require rest. If you work like it all depends on you, then you'll eventually, if not quickly, run out of resources to give. But if you stop and let God refill you, you'll never run dry.

Respect your body's limitations, and find what I like to call "the pace of grace." This is simply your best, natural rhythm based on what you know about yourself and how you function best. Maybe you're a morning person, or you know that you need protein in your breakfast to stay energized throughout your day. It might be knowing when you need to stay in and spend some quiet time alone, and when you need to be with others. Or knowing when you need to rest—which is why God commanded us to take a sabbath.

KEEP THE SABBATH

One crucial way to keep the pace of grace is to practice keeping the Sabbath. This isn't just a good idea—it's one of the Ten Commandments! "You have six days in which to do your work, but the seventh day is a day of rest dedicated to me" (Exodus 20:9–10 GNT).

While your sabbath doesn't have to be the seventh day of the week, or Sunday, I encourage you to designate one day a week as a day of sacred rest. This means not working—nope, not even returning email! When you take a sabbath, you intentionally stop and unplug from your normal routines and activities. No surfing online, no texting, no phone, no social media. Instead, you focus on your relationship with God, perhaps through an extended prayer time or by fasting or by feasting on God's Word.

Sabbath allows you time to rest your body, to enjoy quiet solitude, and to catch up on sleep. This time also allows you to recharge your soul and do things that refuel your tank. It might be enjoying a meal with friends or participating in a communal event. It might be painting or walking along the beach or listening to special music. However you decide to spend your sabbath time, it should feed your soul.

You might use your sabbath time as an opportunity to review and reflect on other areas of your life. You might even take a sabbatical, a period of rest and renewal that's longer than just a day. Whether it's for a week, several weeks, a month, or longer, a sabbatical gives your spirit time to breathe and refocus on what's most important.

A few years ago, I finally took my first extended sabbatical, and it was truly life-changing. No email, no internet, no social media, very few work responsibilities, and limited use of my phone. It was tough at first, because, like most of us, I'm used to being on the go. Actually having time to do nothing was hard! Soon, though, my body began to benefit from catching up on sleep. I was able to slow down and enjoy being present with my family. During my sabbatical, I realized I needed to change the way I typically traveled and scheduled my time.

You may think you don't have time to put your life on hold and practice the Sabbath, let alone take a full sabbatical, but if you want to grow spiritually, as well as in all other areas of your life, then rest isn't optional—it's essential. Take time to rest before you're forced to take time to rest!

GROW IN FAVOR WITH GOD AND MAN

In addition to growing intellectually and physically, Jesus grew "in favor with God and man" (Luke 2:52). This kind of growth implies we're designed to change and grow through our relationships. Obviously, you want to focus on your relationship with God—that's what this book is all about!

Just as you need to be deliberate about spending time with God—praying, worshipping, learning, listening—you also need to be intentional about investing in your relationships with the key people in your life. It's so easy in our busyness to skate on the surface of relationships, even with people we love and want to enjoy. If we're not deliberate about nurturing close relationships, we can accidentally insulate ourselves from a crucial component of our personal growth. We see this contrast revealed in Jesus' visit with two of his friends:

> As Jesus and his disciples were on their way, he came to a village where a woman named Martha opened her home to him. She had a sister called Mary, who sat at the Lord's feet listening to what he said. But Martha was distracted by all the preparations that had to be made. She came to him and asked, "Lord, don't you care that my sister has left me to do the work by myself? Tell her to help me!"
>
> "Martha, Martha," the Lord answered, "you are worried and upset about many things, but few things are needed—or indeed only one. Mary has chosen what is better, and it will not be taken away from her." (Luke 10:38–42)

Notice that Martha was focused on serving Jesus but was not focused on Jesus—visiting with him, talking with and listening to him, just being with him. Mary, on the other hand, didn't worry about preparations, because she wanted to focus all her attention on the precious, limited time she had with her Friend. Their choices remind us that our real friends don't want to critique our cooking so much as they just want to connect with us.

Connecting takes time and attention. Last year I traveled with a group of friends to Scotland where we enjoyed playing golf at St. Andrews, one of the oldest, most iconic courses in the world. While the opportunity to play on such a special course was amazing, what I enjoyed most was the time spent with my buddies when we weren't playing golf!

The best part was our meals together. We'd have dinner and just sit and talk. We spent hours enjoying delicious food and discussing anything and everything—our relationships with God, our families, our struggles, our dreams. We inspired and challenged one another to keep growing, to keep giving everything we have, to trust God more than ever.

Just as a plant requires water, sun, and nutrients from the soil to grow, we require several key elements to grow spiritually. As we cultivate a deeper relationship with God by spending time with him, we also focus on areas contributing to a healthy, balanced life. We see these areas exemplified in the ways Jesus grew—in wisdom, in stature, in favor with God and others—and this model continues to serve us well on our spiritual journey.

If we're not growing, then we're resigning ourselves to stagnation, apathy, and a diminished life. But this is not God's intention for his children! Jesus told us he came to bring us life to the full, overflowing with joy, peace, passion, and purpose. No matter where we are in our spiritual journey, God always provides room for us to grow!

YOUR NEXT STEP ON THE JOURNEY

Disturb us, Lord, when we are too well pleased with ourselves, when our dreams have come true because we have dreamed too little, when we arrived safely because we sailed too close to the shore.

—Sir Francis Drake, 1577

We don't have to be world explorers like Sir Francis Drake to enjoy the adventure of personal growth. I've discovered that I'm happiest when I'm aware that I'm being deliberate about trying to grow. When I'm pursuing a new goal, stepping out of my usual comfort zone, or practicing a new discipline, I enjoy actively growing in my faith.

Years ago, I started a practice I learned from another pastor. Once a month, I take a personal retreat day to evaluate what's going on in all the areas of my life. Just as with car engines and home care, preventive maintenance is so much easier to do than full-scale repairs. So, every month I look at a dozen different areas of my life—sort of like the indicators on a car's dashboard—and grade myself in each one. Then I write one sentence about how I can improve in that area in the month to come. Here are the twelve areas I focus on:

1. **Faith life:** How is my relationship with God?
2. **Marriage life:** How is my relationship with Tammy?
3. **Family life:** How are my relationships with my kids and immediate family?
4. **Office life:** How much time do I spend there, and is it effective?
5. **Computer life:** How can I productively spend less time on it?
6. **Ministry life:** How can I touch the lives of others? Where do I give?
7. **Financial life:** How are my personal finances?
8. **Social life:** When am I spending time engaged with friends?
9. **Attitudinal life:** Overall, what's my attitude lately?
10. **Creative life:** Am I dreaming? Writing?
11. **Travel life:** How do I balance time away from home and church?
12. **Physical life:** Am I taking care of my body and physical self?

You don't have to use these particular twelve, but I encourage you to look at your life and come up with the major areas that consume your time most days right now. List them and give yourself a score on how you're doing in each one, with 1 being "not well at all" and 10 being "great—couldn't be better." What patterns do you notice? What areas are thriving? What areas need critical attention right away? Make an appointment with yourself to review your list of areas and update your growth in the next month.

Remember, happiness is growth, so never stop growing!

MAKE A DIFFERENCE

As our five adult children continue to spread their wings, our family tries to get together at least once a month for a meal. Two of our kids still live at home, three are married, and we're blessed to have five grandchildren, so getting us all in one place at one time can be a challenge. We usually meet at a favorite restaurant, which the kids like because they know Dad will pay. My wife and I like it, because we're committed to keeping our family connected.

Recently, we all agreed to meet at P. F. Chang's, and the place was packed. Tammy had made a reservation, fortunately, so we didn't have to wait to be seated, but the service was uncharacteristically slow. Now, I can be a demanding customer just as easily as anyone else, but that night I was in a different kind of mood. I felt content to just enjoy the time together to talk and catch up with everyone, waiting patiently to order our meals.

When our server finally arrived, she seemed especially frantic. Her face held that "I have way too many tables" look we've all seen before. I felt sympathetic toward her and said, "We're in no hurry, so don't worry about us. Go ahead and take care of your other tables." Tammy and our kids looked at me like I'd lost my mind, and our waitress looked just as surprised. But I felt like she needed someone to care about her in a place where most people tend to care only about themselves. She thanked me but proceeded to take our orders.

While two or three different conversations began around our table, my mind lingered on our waitress. I wondered what her life was like. Maybe she was working several jobs to get through college. Maybe she was a single mom worried about providing for her kids. Maybe she had something going on in her personal life. Or maybe she was just exhausted from a long shift on a busy night. For some reason, I wanted to show her kindness and compassion. I wanted her to know that someone, even if I was only her customer, cared about her.

Shortly after our food arrived, she came around to check on us, but I turned the tables on her and asked, "Are *you* okay?"

She looked at me with a puzzled expression.

"I'm a pastor," I added, refusing to break eye contact.

Her eyes immediately misted with tears. Then she regained her composure and said, "Just pray for me," before she scurried to another table. I nodded that I would, knowing I was "all in" at this point. Clearly, something weighed on her heart.

After my family went through enough lettuce wraps, Kung Pao chicken, and fried rice to feed an army, I asked for the check, already feeling compelled to leave a generous gratuity despite the slow service. In fact, I wanted to leave a tip that would get her attention. One that she would think was a mistake because it was so generous.

Now, don't go thinking I'm some big spender, because I normally just leave the usual percentage like most people.

Sure enough, just as we were leaving our table, she came rushing toward me with the little leather check portfolio in hand. "Sir, I think you made a mistake," she said, opening the bill to show me the number she assumed was an error.

I smiled and said, "No, we're all set. That's for you."

Tears threatened to spill from her eyes once again. "Why?" she asked.

"God wanted me to tell you that he loves you."

"You have no idea what this means," she whispered before she turned and walked away.

I had hoped the money I left would be a blessing to her. But realizing that God had given me the privilege of leaving it for her was a blessing to me. Driving home that night, I felt an incredible sense of fulfillment. I was reminded that we're all here on this earth to minister to one another. God calls each of us to be an agent of his healing in a broken world. If we're willing to listen and pay attention, he reveals such opportunities every day.

The purpose of life is to discover your gift.

The meaning of life is to give your gift away.

COMPLETE JOY

With more than seven billion people on the planet, God chose me to make a difference in the life of one of his precious children—a waitress in a busy restaurant. I easily could have been frustrated and impatient, as I often am. But for some reason, that night I was aware of wanting to surprise someone with a glimpse of God's love. I couldn't solve all her problems or become her counselor. But I could leave a tip big enough for it to be conspicuous.

This is the privilege we all have—to serve one another and make a difference. Jesus said, "This is to my Father's glory, that you bear much fruit, showing yourselves to be my disciples. . . . I have told you this so that my joy may be in you and that your joy may be complete" (John 15:8, 11). Notice this isn't just a command from the Lord; it's a recipe for lasting joy!

Real joy does not come from making a lot of money.
Real joy does not come from having a lot of physical pleasure.
Real joy does not come from possessing a lot of material things.
Real joy comes from knowing your life is productive.
Real joy springs from knowing you're making a difference for eternity!

Knowing that you're living out your God-given purpose and that you're making a difference in other people's lives for all eternity changes your focus. You begin living your life beyond yourself and your own comfort and convenience. You become a conduit of God's love, grace, mercy, and generosity: "God has given each of you a gift from his great variety of spiritual gifts. Use them well to serve one another" (1 Peter 4:10 NLT).

Generous people are happy people. The Greek word *makarios* is often translated "blessed" in the Bible, but it literally means "happy." This feeling is not just an emotional reaction—it's also physical. A few years back I read an article in the *Wall Street Journal* reporting on a medical study that discovered acts of generosity release neurochemicals in our brains that bring pleasure.[1] God created our bodies to enjoy giving to others! "The generous will prosper; those who refresh others will themselves be refreshed" (Proverbs 11:25 NLT).

You are part of God's plan.

You can make a difference.

That's why you're here!

CHAPTER TEN

SERVANT HEART

THE GREATEST OF ALL TIME

N o, I disagree—nobody comes close to Jack Nicklaus in his prime!"

"But compare the number of tournament titles, and Tiger has to be the greatest!"

"You're both wrong! It's Arnold Palmer without a doubt!"

I can't tell you how often I've overheard—and sometimes been part of—conversations like this coming off the golf course. It's the kind of debate you often hear among sports enthusiasts. Whether it's motivated by love of the game or an appreciation of the talent and level of experience required to win championships, tournaments, titles, and MVP awards, most fans are quick to defend their selection for the GOAT, the Greatest of All Time.

The debate often includes a review of the amazing talent of current athletes as compared to stars of the past. Who's greater on the tennis court, Martina Navratilova or Serena Williams? In the boxing ring, do you go with Muhammad Ali or Floyd Mayweather? LeBron James or Michael Jordan? Cristiano Ronaldo or Pelé? Joe Montana or Tom Brady? On and on the comparisons go, but these debates will never be settled.

Most of us will never have to worry about being the greatest professional athlete. You may wonder, however, how you stack up against others in your office, department, or team. You may even struggle with comparing yourself to others in your neighborhood, school, or church community. While we all struggle with wanting recognition for who we are and what we do, in life there's no debate about who's the greatest.

Jesus settled it once and for all.

THE FIRST WILL BE LAST

Wanting to be recognized as a Very Important Person is nothing new. Even the disciples of Jesus argued over who was the greatest among them. Most of them likely expected Jesus to overthrow the Roman occupation of Israel and usher in a new government. Just like political players today, the disciples consequently began jockeying for power. They wanted an important role in what they assumed would be the new order once Jesus became king. Which makes me wonder if they were confused by the counterintuitive command their Master gave them:

> Jesus called them together and said, "You know that those who are regarded as rulers of the Gentiles lord it over them, and their high officials exercise authority over them. Not so with you. Instead, whoever wants to become great among you must be your servant, and whoever wants to be first must be slave of all. For even the Son of Man did not come to be served, but to serve, and to give his life as a ransom for many." (Mark 10:42–45)

Both the Jewish religious authorities and the Roman government of Jesus' day relied on a hierarchy of power. Then, as now, people abused their authority and often manipulated others toward their own personal agendas, often for money or more power. Those in charge decided what the rest of the citizens had to do to survive.

With this kind of mindset in place, along with the expectation that Jesus would rule an earthly kingdom, Jesus' followers probably couldn't wait until they had their turn to change the system. They may even have been well-intentioned, hoping to correct past injustices. So, when Jesus told them that the greatest leaders must be

the greatest servants—including himself as an example—
his words must have blown their minds. Not only would
they not be holding positions of government or religious
authority, but they were called to serve everyone else!

This exchange was not an isolated incident. Over
and over, Jesus taught this important principle. He even
taught it one last time the night before he went to the
cross. Let's pick up the story in John 13:

> It was just before the Passover Festival. Jesus knew that
> the hour had come for him to leave this world and go
> to the Father. Having *loved* his own who were in the
> world, he *loved* them to the end. (v.1, my emphasis)

Before Jesus showed his followers the extent of his
love by dying on the cross, he demonstrated it in another
way. The night before he was crucified, Christ and his
disciples gathered together for the Passover meal, which
became known to us as the Last Supper. As part of any
host's courtesy to his or her guests, someone, usually a
servant or slave, would be designated to wash everyone
else's feet.

Only no one had volunteered ahead of time or
arranged for a servant to come wash their feet. No one
wanted to do such a humbling—arguably, *humiliating*—
job as soaking and sudsing others' dirty feet (remember,
people in those days typically wore sandals or no shoes
at all). Washing feet was the minimum-wage job of that

time—even servants found it disgusting. With none of the disciples willing to do it, they decided to proceed with the Passover meal. But the tension lingered and led to an argument over who among them was greatest.

We can only imagine how Jesus must have felt seeing his closest friends bicker among themselves. We can almost imagine him thinking, *Haven't they learned anything from being with me?* Some of the disciples even suggested getting their mother involved to pressure Jesus into recognizing them as the greatest. But beneath the surface of all this bickering and jockeying for power, Jesus knew that one of them, Judas, was about to betray him. Christ also knew that Peter would go on to deny him within the next twenty-four hours.

While the disciples continued eating, arguing, and outdoing each other, Jesus quietly stood up, removed his outer cloak, got a basin of water and a towel, and began washing their feet. Some, like Peter, protested and refused to let Jesus do it, but their Master made it clear that if they truly loved him and considered him their Lord, then they would have to receive the gift of service he was performing.

Jesus then revealed that he was setting an example for them: "Now that I, your Lord and Teacher, have washed your feet, you also should wash one another's feet. I have set you an example that *you should do as I have done for you*" (vv. 14–15, my emphasis). Jesus plainly and unapologetically called his followers then and every one of us now to a life of servanthood. We are to be the first to act, to serve, to do what no one else is willing to do.

Our example is not only to make a point, however. When we serve, we receive the hidden benefit of giving to others. Jesus explained, "Now that you know these things, you will be blessed if you do them" (v. 17). Not only do we benefit from giving all we can give, but we also have the privilege of drawing closer to Christ and the example he set for us. The more we serve, the more we want to serve!

SERVE TO MAGNIFY

If servanthood is a hallmark of a believer, then we need to understand it well. While it may seem simple enough at first glance, there are actually seven different Greek words in the New Testament for the word *servant*. Let's consider three of them that shed more light on this unique aspect of our faith.

Addressing his disciples, Jesus used a term that literally means "bondservant," from the Greek word *doulos*: "Sitting down, Jesus called the Twelve and said, 'Anyone who wants to be first must be the very last, and the servant of all'" (Mark 9:35). In the cultural context of that time, a bondservant was a "bound" servant. These were people who became so indebted that they were forced to become servants to their creditors. While Jewish law allowed them to serve for only seven years, many of these servants became attached to their masters and continued to work for them after that time. Many, to indicate their lifetime devotion to their masters, pierced their ears with an awl. Consequently, we're reminded that our devotion to God is a lifetime commitment.

In another Gospel account, the Greek word *diakonos* is used: "Whoever wants to become great among you must be your servant, and whoever wants to be first must be your slave" (Matthew 20:26–27). This usage literally translates as "deacon" rather than just "servant" and originally referred to the seven men who were assigned to wait on guests at dinners and holiday meals. Like waiters at a restaurant, these deacons made sure guests had a wonderful experience. The concept reminds us to take the focus off ourselves and serve the people around us.

Finally, we find one of my favorites, the Greek word *huperetes*, which literally translates as "under-rower." We see it used when Paul describes his own conversion experience: "Now get up and stand on your feet. I have appeared to you to appoint you as a servant and as a witness of what you have seen and will see of me" (Acts 26:16).

An *under-rower* refers to the kind of servants and slaves working on a Roman ship, usually as oarsmen to power the vessel. You may remember in *Ben Hur* that slaves, chained to the oars beneath the main deck, could "row and live." These under-rowers remained anonymous, the unseen force propelling the boat, a reminder that our goal is to magnify Jesus, not ourselves. We do this by helping others shine without claiming credit.

Why do I especially appreciate these forms of servant-hood? Because they fit together to remind us of what it means to be a true servant: a lifetime commitment to serve people's needs in such a way as to magnify Jesus!

HEART OF A SERVANT

While being a servant isn't easy, nothing is more beautiful than seeing people give themselves to the needs of others. Like the CEO who rolls up her sleeves and pitches in to get the envelopes stuffed in the mailroom when she finds the intern overwhelmed by such a task. Or the young teen willing to mow the grass or shovel the sidewalk for his elderly neighbor without being asked. The couple will-ing to sacrifice their long-awaited vacation in order to help feed and shelter people in their city devastated by a hurricane.

When you see someone serving like Jesus, you're inspired to do the same. And while there's no formula for how to grow in our willingness to serve, I've noticed some traits that most Christ-like servers seem to share. Each of these qualities reflects a different facet of God's good-ness and Jesus' sacrificial love. Each one reminds us to take our eyes off ourselves, off our own self-importance, off our own needs and desires. Instead, we see the needs around us and give all we have to provide what God has so generously provided for us.

1. A SERVANT PUTS SERVICE OVER STATUS.

We all have to fight against the gravitational pull of selfishness. It's human nature. Whether it's a baby crying to be fed or an office manager manipulating others for a promotion, we all want what we want when we want it. To be effective and impactful servants, we usually have to fight this tendency to focus on our own interests. The Bible tells us, "Do nothing out of *selfish* ambition or vain conceit. Rather, in humility value others *above yourselves*, not looking to your own interests but each of you to the *interests of the others*" (Philippians 2:3–4, my emphasis).

Servants know that what they're doing is not about them but about others. Following the example of Jesus, we don't serve to get credit or praise, a PR boost or a photo op. In fact, most servants prefer to work anonymously, like the under-rowers, behind the scenes where no one sees what they're doing. They don't want their names mentioned or their performance noticed.

Working toward this goal, we try to strike a balance in our church between having a presence in our community so that people see us and know what we're about, and refraining from showboating in the ways we give, serve, and contribute. We want everything we do to be for the glory of Christ, not for the glory of Church of the Highlands and most certainly not for the glory of Chris Hodges or any other individual or group.

2. A SERVANT PUTS CHARACTER OVER COMFORT.

True servants of Jesus have integrity. They make decisions born out of their obedience to God's Word, to their conscience, and to the prompting of the Holy Spirit. They do what's right, not what's convenient or easy. In fact, good servers know the truth—serving is *never* convenient!

Jesus told a parable that makes this point in capital letters. The story of the good Samaritan is all about convenience:

> "There was once a man traveling from Jerusalem to Jericho. On the way he was attacked by robbers. They took his clothes, beat him up, and went off leaving him half-dead. Luckily, a priest was on his way down the same road, but when he saw him he angled across to the other side. Then a Levite religious man showed up; he also avoided the injured man.
>
> A Samaritan traveling the road came on him. When he saw the man's condition, his heart went out to him. He gave him first aid, disinfecting and bandaging his wounds. Then he lifted him onto his donkey, led him to an inn, and made him comfortable. In the

morning he took out two silver coins and gave them to the innkeeper, saying, 'Take good care of him. If it costs any more, put it on my bill—I'll pay you on my way back.'

"What do you think? Which of the three became a neighbor to the man attacked by robbers?"

"The one who treated him kindly," the religion scholar responded.

Jesus said, "Go and do the same." (Luke 10:30–37 THE MESSAGE)

I love what Dr. Martin Luther King Jr. pointed out about this parable. Both the priest and the Levite asked, "If I stop to help this man, what effect will it have on *me*? What's the cost if I give and serve this need?" They were thinking only about how it would inconvenience them. The good Samaritan, however, reversed the question: "If I don't stop to help this man, what will happen to *him*?"

Have you ever thought that? You find out about some problem or need, and you simply can't keep living without doing something?

I think of people like Lee and Laura Domingue, who were on a trip overseas when they learned about the horrors of human trafficking. They simply couldn't have peace knowing of the atrocities faced by women, men, and children being bought and sold around the world. So, the Domingues began doing what they could do, partnering with other ministries and nonprofits. Their passion for ending this problem eventually inspired them to create their own nonprofit called Trafficking Hope (www.traffickinghope.com).

Maybe you simply can't stand the thought of people going hungry in your city. Or based on your past struggles and what you've learned, you now have a burden to help others get out of debt. No matter what it is, when you discover a need, an issue, a problem, an injustice that grips your heart, you have an opportunity to be a good Samaritan. To put Christ before convenience. To put others before self.

Stop asking yourself what you will lose or what it will cost if you help someone. Start asking what will happen to someone if you don't help them. If you don't do it, who will?

3. A SERVANT PUTS "WE" OVER "ME."

Sometimes being a Christ-like servant means collaborating instead of doing it yourself. This can be tough, especially if you're an independent, self-sufficient type of person who likes to take charge and get things done. "If you want something done right, do it yourself!" is your motto. But instead of trying to do everything yourself, you will likely have to learn to be part of a team.

As we discussed previously, no part of the body can exist independently of the other parts. All the parts function together as one whole. This is especially true for the body of Christ and our ability to accomplish more together than individually: "All the believers were *together* and had everything in *common*. They sold property and possessions to *give* to anyone who had need" (Acts 2:44–45, my emphasis).

There is simply no way that my family and I, or anyone else I know, could have the kind of impact we're creating by coming together at our church. I'm so glad to be part of this church, this community, this family of believers that wants to pool resources and do together what we could never do alone.

4. A SERVANT PUTS WORSHIP OVER WEALTH.

This final quality of a true servant motivates me the most. It challenges us to be stewards and use what we have for the good of others and the glory of God. In Scripture we read:

> "When the Son of Man comes in his glory, and all the angels with him, he will sit on his glorious throne. All the nations will be gathered before him, and he will separate the people one from another as a shepherd separates the sheep from the goats. He will put the sheep on his right and the goats on his left.
>
> "Then the King will say to those on his right, 'Come, you who are blessed by my Father; *take your inheritance*, the kingdom prepared for you since the creation of the world. For I was hungry and you gave me something to eat, I was thirsty and you gave me

something to drink, I was a stranger and you invited me in, I needed clothes and you clothed me, I was sick and you looked after me, I was in prison and you came to visit me.'" (Matthew 25:31–36, my emphasis)

Notice how incredibly practical Jesus is here! As his followers, we take our inheritance and use it to meet the physical needs around us. If we see someone hungry, we feed them. If someone is thirsty, we give them a drink. If they're sick, we take care of them. Whatever the need is before us, we are called to meet it. Because when we meet the needs of other people, we're also serving God:

"Then the righteous will answer him, 'Lord, when did we see you hungry and feed you, or thirsty and give you something to drink? When did we see you a stranger and invite you in, or needing clothes and clothe you? When did we see you sick or in prison and go to visit you?'

"The King will reply, 'Truly I tell you, whatever you did for one of *the least of these* brothers and sisters of mine, you did for *me*.'" (vv. 37–40, my emphasis)

We're not just doing it for the person we're serving; we're doing it for the Lord. As servants we realize that we can take what we have—our time, our money, our possessions—and use it to bless others. We're not only meeting their needs and blessing them, we're also worshipping the source of our love, generosity, and provision. Serving is one of the highest forms of worship.

I've been reminded of this truth as I've watched my kids grow up. As many siblings do, my children have often fussed and fought over silly things. But even when their relationships with one another have become strained, they've continued to love their mother and me. Consequently, as they've gotten older, they've realized that when they love each other, they're also loving their parents. They've learned that they can't love me without loving the people I love!

Serving others is serving God.

How you serve is how you worship.

YOUR NEXT STEP ON
THE JOURNEY

If you want to grow in your faith, then make a commitment to serve. It doesn't have to be big, dramatic, or profound—in fact, it may be better if it's not. You simply need to find a need and fill it or find a hurt and heal it. If you're not sure what you can do, ask around at your local church, school, food bank, shelter, or senior citizens center. See how you can be the hands and feet of Jesus for people in your community.

Be willing to do whatever needs doing without resisting, complaining, or giving it a second thought. Be the one who does what others aren't willing to do. Be a foot washer, an under-rower, a bondservant. Read to children in the hospital. Wash windows and clean gutters for the elderly. Tutor teens who need help with their writing. Prepare a meal for someone dealing with a family crisis. Collect winter coats, hats, and gloves for the homeless in your area. With access to the internet and social media, most of us don't have an excuse for finding a need to fill.

Make whatever you choose to do an act of worship, an offering to God. Use it as an opportunity to reflect on the many blessings in your life even as you bless others around you. Give of yourself without expecting anything in return.

Just like Jesus.

CHAPTER ELEVEN

ETERNAL REWARD

TREASURES IN HEAVEN

I hate tests.

In school growing up, I knew I was smarter than my test scores revealed. Almost every time I had to take a test in high school and then into college, I would study and prepare until I felt confident. Even after taking those tests, I often felt good about my performance—until I got them back with a grade of C or even D. I knew the material, I studied hard, and yet I still couldn't do well at exam time. It just didn't make sense!

Once I started at Louisiana State University, I hoped my experience with tests might be different. But it was just the opposite. I soon hated tests more than ever, especially multiple choice. Maybe it's just my personality or the way I think, but I could make a case for almost every possible answer offered on a multiple-choice quiz. I felt tricked or even deceived when I'd get my grade and see the "right" answers.

My frustration finally became fruitful during my second year at LSU. A classmate let me in on what was apparently a well-known secret: the campus bookstore sold copies of old tests for many of the core classes. For around a buck apiece, I could purchase previous exams and see the types of questions asked. I could learn the professors' perspectives and the way they wanted their students to analyze the material. Some of the questions and essay prompts even got recycled and popped up on the very tests I was taking.

From that point on, I made an A on every test I took. My grade point average quickly climbed to 4.0. I knew what to expect, so taking the exam was a breeze. It's always easier to pass a test if you know what's required of you.

TESTS IN ETERNITY

There's going to be a test in eternity, and I want you to be ready. But don't stress, because not only am I going to tell you what the test covers, I'm also going to give you the answers. In fact, there are really two tests, two moments when we will come before God and be evaluated. If you don't understand the two tests, and the difference between them, then the Bible can seem confusing, even contradictory.

These tests reflect what was important to us during our time on earth. They reveal how we invested our time, our talents, and our treasure. Did we pour all we had into an eternal legacy to make a difference for God's kingdom? Or did we squander our gifts and miss opportunities to bless others as we were blessed?

THE FIRST TEST

The first test is one that everyone who has ever lived will take. From the beginning of time until the very end, every person will come before God. This encounter is often called the Great White Throne Judgment based on John's prophetic vision recorded in Revelation:

> Then I saw a great white throne and him who was seated on it. The earth and the heavens fled from his presence, and there was no place for them. And I saw the dead, great and small, standing before the throne, and books were opened. Another book was opened, which is the book of life. The dead were judged according to what they had done as recorded in the books. (Revelation 20:11–12)

Notice here two separate references, one to "books" (plural) and one to "book" (singular). The plural books record everything anyone ever did, right or wrong, good or bad. And, of course, it only takes one mistake to be imperfect, unholy, a sinner. Every sin leads to death and requires atonement, a price to be paid.

The singular book, however—the "book of life"—records the names of those people who have surrendered their lives to Jesus as Lord and Savior. He is the only one who can pay for your sin, so you don't have to try. Your debt is canceled, and your relationship with God is restored. This book, also known as the Lamb's Book of Life, includes the names of all those who accept this gift of grace. Instead of receiving an eternal death sentence for your sins, you experience new life in Christ.

The first test in eternity, therefore, is quite simple. There's only one question God will ask you, and I suspect it will be something like, "What did you do with my Son, Jesus?" Before we explore the response required to pass this test, though, let's look at some wrong answers.

"Uh, I went to church and sang all those worship songs about Jesus!"

"I read the Bible every day and studied so many books about your Son's life."

"I believed Jesus really is your Son."

"Well, Jesus really inspired me. I volunteered so much time in that urban ministry and gave lots of money to help those in need."

All wrong answers! Surprised? These all include good things to do, but none of them reflect the sole answer at the heart of what God wants to know. While we may be tempted to think we'll be judged based on what we do, Jesus made it clear this will not be the case:

> "Not everyone who says to me, 'Lord, Lord,' will enter the kingdom of heaven, but only the one who does the will of my Father who is in heaven. Many will say to me on that day, 'Lord, Lord, did we not prophesy in your name and in your name drive out demons and in your name perform many miracles?' Then I will tell them plainly, 'I never knew you. Away from me, you evildoers!'" (Matthew 7:21–23)

So, what's the *right* answer? "I know Jesus personally. We have a close relationship. I love him because of how much he first loved me. I'm so not worthy—no one is—but I'm a sinner saved by grace and grace alone."

All eternity is based on a *relationship* with Jesus—not religion.

It's who you know, not what you do.

If you know his Son personally, God will welcome you into his heaven.

It's that simple.

THE SECOND TEST

Now we come to the second test, and many people are surprised by it. They don't realize another judgment occurs after entrance into heaven. This test is an evaluation of how we lived our life and what we did with all that was entrusted to us: "For we must all appear before the judgment seat of Christ, so that each of us may receive what is due us for the things done while in the body, whether good or bad" (2 Corinthians 5:10).

Judgment tends to be such a harsh word, and this test is more of an awards ceremony. It's like the medals podium at the Olympics where the results are revealed, and the bronze, silver, and gold medals are awarded. No one will be unhappy or disappointed here—this is purely a celebration of what each of us has done to make a difference! We're told, "For the Son of Man is going to come in his Father's glory with his angels, and then he will reward each person according to what they have done" (Matthew 16:27).

Jesus is excited about giving you an award for how you lived your life. He wants to review your works with you and reward you accordingly. "Look, I am coming soon! My reward is with me, and I will give to each person according to what they have done" (Revelation 22:12).

You may be thinking, *But isn't heaven enough of a reward in itself?* True, it certainly is. But God's nature is the essence of generosity. It's simply who he is.

I imagine God's question at this second test to be something like, "What did you do with all that I gave you?" I tend to think of it as similar to the way the master of the house returns in Jesus' parable of the talents (Matthew 25:14–30). It's a time of reckoning, a time to go over the return you made on God's resources. He gives us so much—energy, time, skills, opportunities, ideas, talents, money, relationships, on and on. While he loves to bless us and wants us to enjoy his gifts, God also expects a return on his investment. He expects us to leverage all that is entrusted to us to make a difference for eternity.

You see, everything we have—everything we are—is a gift from God to be used for his glory. The answer you and I want to give is the same one God wants to hear: "I used all you gave me to make a difference for eternity."

ALL THAT REMAINS

I sincerely hope you're ready for the first test, and if you've made it this far in the book, I'm guessing you are. But I want to challenge you to consider how you will fare with the second test. Will your life's work survive? No matter your answer, if you've accepted Jesus as your Savior, you will still go to heaven—that's a free gift and can't be earned. But like getting an advanced degree, after passing the first test, you should feel more motivated to pass the second. Paul explains this in his letter to members of the early church at Corinth:

> For we are co-workers in God's service; you are God's field, God's building.
>
> By the grace God has given me, I laid a foundation

as a wise builder, and someone else is building on it. But each one should build with care. For no one can lay any foundation other than the one already laid, which is Jesus Christ. If anyone builds on this foundation using gold, silver, costly stones, wood, hay or straw, their work will be shown for what it is, because the Day will bring it to light. It will be revealed with fire, and the fire will test the quality of each person's work. If what has been built survives, the builder will receive a reward. If it is burned up, the builder will suffer loss but yet will be saved—even though only as one escaping through the flames. (1 Corinthians 3:9–15)

Have you ever witnessed the aftermath of a major fire? You might recall as I do seeing the charred remains of forests, homes, and buildings after the deadly wildfires our country has experienced in recent years. So much stuff reduced to ashes. Millions if not billions of dollars' worth of material possessions lost—making whatever did survive that much more precious and valuable.

The fire mentioned in Paul's letter similarly has the power to destroy as well as to reveal all that remains. "On the judgment day, fire will reveal what kind of work each builder has done. The fire will show if a person's work has any value. If the work *survives*, that builder will receive a reward. But if the work is burned up, the builder will suffer great loss. The builder will be saved, but like someone barely escaping through a wall of flames" (vv. 13–15 NLT, my emphasis). This passage explains the relationship between the two tests. If you pass the first, you'll end up in heaven no matter how your life's work gets evaluated. But if you pass the second, if your work endures in heaven, you'll receive God's reward. If we've accepted Jesus into our lives, then we pass the first test. From this group of test passers, however, different people will receive different rewards based on how they invested what God gave them.

Let's be people who keep both rewards in mind as we pursue God's work.

GIVE BEYOND

If you want to invest in eternity and pass the second test with flying colors, then never forget the value of what God has given you. Remember, what we do for ourselves usually dies with us. But what we do for others lives beyond us.

The best way to live your life is to invest in something that will outlast your time on earth. Consider how the psalmist describes the kind of person who does this: "Good will come to those who are generous and lend freely, who conduct their affairs with justice. Surely the righteous will never be shaken; they will be remembered forever" (Psalm 112:5–6). And here's how the same psalmist describes a righteous person's legacy: "They share freely and give generously to those in need. Their good deeds will be remembered forever. They will have influence and honor" (v. 9 NLT).

Keep in mind that it's not all about money. You can be rich and generous in so many other ways. The Bible makes this clear: "You will be *enriched in every way* so that you can be *generous on every occasion*, and through us your generosity will result in thanksgiving to God" (2 Corinthians 9:11, my emphasis). Let's consider a few of the ways you can practice generosity with your resources to make an eternal impact.

1. GIVE YOUR TIME.

For most of us, time is more valuable than money. We all spend our time differently, yet I suspect we all spend too much of it on activities, events, and relationships without much eternal value. If we want what we do today to count for all eternity, then we must be deliberate about how we invest our seconds, minutes, and hours.

Each day, choose to live that day so that it will be remembered in heaven. Serve in your church. Give some hours to community projects. Mentor kids in your neighborhood. Befriend someone who can't get out much. Look for opportunities each day to make your time count for more than your own convenience, comfort, or pleasure.

One of my favorite events at our church is our SERVE

Day. On the first Saturday of each month, we coordinate ways our members can go out into our community and serve the needs of others. We mow yards, repair homes, paint walls, clean up parks, and do whatever we can to show the love of Jesus in practical ways throughout our region. Many of our small groups participate in SERVE Days together so they can share the blessing of blessing others through their efforts.

Such efforts take time—precious free time on most people's days off. But their time gets multiplied into eternity. They will be rewarded.

2. GIVE YOUR TALENT.

We covered this earlier in chapter 10, as well as in our discussion of discovering your purpose in section 2, but now is a great time to consider the way your purpose directly affects others' lives for the kingdom of God. What you do can last beyond your lifetime! Your God-given gifts are not only making a difference for those around you, but for others across time as well.

You have been created uniquely. You are fearfully and wonderfully made. Use your special gifts to draw others to God and his kingdom. Make what you do count for more than your own fulfillment. Join a ministry team—or create one—so you can be sure your service survives forever. Every day make sure you give away your talent to something that matters for eternity.

3. GIVE YOUR TOUCH.

You interact with other people every day—at home, school, work, church, the mall, the grocery store, everywhere. How you interact with them can change the course of their lives forever. A smile, a handshake, an encouraging word, a listening ear, a kind gesture, and a shared laugh have so much power beyond the moment they're given.

Obviously, you want to respect others and not offer any touch that's unwanted or inappropriate. But kindness, patience, and compassion are always welcome. As so many people struggle with frustration, rage, and division in our culture today, we are called to show them the love of Jesus. We are the peacemakers. We bring salt and light.

You reflect God's character, one way or another, every time you interact with another human being. So, make the most of those opportunities! Leave others wondering what you have that makes you so happy to see them.

4. GIVE YOUR TREASURE.

Treasure obviously includes your money, but it also refers to your whole attitude toward finances, possessions, your home, and your lifestyle. Instead of thinking about how little you can give to fulfill your obligation, try to see how much you can give out of the fullness of a generous heart. Keep in mind that what you give to others has a direct effect on what's given to you: "*Give*, and it will be given to you. A good measure, pressed down, shaken together and running over, will be poured into your lap. For *with the measure you use*, it will be measured to you" (Luke 6:38, my emphasis).

My friend, give your life away! Make a difference in the lives of others. Once you begin living generously, you'll discover what life is all about. The value of life is determined not by how much you achieve or accumulate, but by how much of your life you give away.

5. GIVE JESUS.

Probably the most important thing you can do to store up treasure in heaven is to share your faith with someone. Why? Because only people last forever. We are eternal spirits dwelling in temporary bodies. It's up to us to help others discover and accept all that God has for them. "We are Christ's ambassadors; God is making his appeal through us" (2 Corinthians 5:20 NLT).

Jesus encourages us to share our faith with others. His command is often called the Great Commission and reflects his heart for everyone—*every single person*—to know him and his love for them. "Jesus said to his followers, 'Go everywhere in the world, and tell the Good News to everyone'" (Mark 16:15 NCV).

If you really care about others, then you want them to know what you have in your relationship with God. You want to help them remove whatever obstacles are in the way so they can open their hearts to God's Spirit. You want them to experience the irrational, illogical, unconditional love of God in undeniable ways. You want to give them Jesus.

YOUR NEXT STEP ON THE JOURNEY

To store up treasure in heaven, you will need to invest in people—all people, especially the ones different from you. The ones who may not understand you or your culture. Who may not trust you or know what motivates you. The ones who watch you to understand what following Jesus is all about. So, what can you do? How can you help them?

Give them time, attention, value.
Show them love, understanding, acceptance.
Share your hope, your church, your faith in Jesus
  with them.

Another way to store up treasure in heaven is to regularly assess how you're stewarding what you've been given. Accountants, financial analysts, and stockbrokers often review portfolios to see how various investments are performing. They also perform audits to determine the overall worth of the entire portfolio. I encourage you to do the same with the portfolio of your eternal investments. What have you been doing that God will recognize in heaven at your second judgment? What else would you like to do? Spend some time in prayer, and ask the Holy Spirit to reveal how to invest your time, talent, and earthly treasure in order to reap rewards in heaven.

Finally, look for opportunities to be more deliberate in sharing your faith. Most people don't want you to use a tract or immediately quote Bible verses. They may even be reluctant to talk about God or what they believe about spiritual things. Allow God's Spirit to guide you in your conversations and interactions. Be yourself. Answer honestly and openly. Tell them you don't have all the answers, but you know Someone who does. Let them see Jesus through you.

To help you in this endeavor, I encourage you to write down the names of three people you already know for whom you want to pray regarding their salvation.

Pray for them each day for at least a month, and pay attention to opportunities to serve them and love them without necessarily talking about your faith. Trust that the right time will present itself when they will be ready to talk directly about Jesus and what it means to know him. Above all, don't pressure yourself to do any of these things out of obligation. When I take out the trash, get the oil changed in Tammy's car, or surprise her by cooking dinner, I do it because I love her. I know I'm showing her my love and investing in the quality of our marriage. Our relationship with God should be the same way. Be motivated by his love to pursue these things that please him, and allow God to work through you as you invest in people, steward what you've been given, and share your faith. Someday, you will be elated to hear him say, "Well done, my good and faithful servant. You are my beloved child, and in you I am most pleased!"

CHAPTER TWELVE

IMPACT

CHANGE YOUR WORLD

What's wrong with you, Chris? Don't you want a drink?" my buddy said, pulling out a bottle of whiskey.

"Yeah, Chris—what's up with you? You've been acting funny for a while now," said my other friend.

I was fifteen years old and had been a Christian for only a few weeks. My three best buddies and I were on a field trip with our school choir, competing in a city about four hours from our hometown. The trip required an overnight stay in a hotel, and the four of us were rooming together.

We had been hanging out together for more than five years at that point. We played in a rock band together.

No one had ever invited us to play anywhere, but it was an excuse to get together and jam—and, as we got older, to drink, smoke, and see how much trouble we could get into. We also took choir, partly because we loved music but mostly for an easy A.

But now that I was a Christian, our old pursuits didn't interest me—well, except for music. Instead, God had given me a burden to reach my best friends and tell them what had happened in my heart. Knowing we would room together and have plenty of time to talk, I had prayed for the courage to speak up. Once curfew sent us to our rooms, my buddies hauled out the liquor and cigars and a deck of cards. They were ready to kick back like we'd always done before. Scared and excited, I could hear my heart drumming in my ears faster and louder than a Phil Collins drum solo.

"Uh, guys," I said. "Can we talk for a minute? I want to tell you what's been going on and haven't had a good chance until now."

They looked at each other and then back at me before nodding in unison. Relieved that they were at least willing to listen, I launched into a rambling summary of what I'd experienced the past few weeks. I told them about giving my life to Jesus and the change it had made in me. I told them I knew without a doubt God was real and wanted to relate to them as his sons. The only verse I could think to quote was Genesis 1:1—"In the beginning God created the heavens and the earth"—and then I jumped from there to how I believed hell was real. As best I could, I explained about sin and how Jesus died on the cross to pay the debt we could never pay ourselves. Out of breath and ready to make my final point, I blurted, "You're my best friends, and I don't want you all to go to hell."

The seconds of silence that followed seemed to last for hours. My mind raced as I thought of things I wished I had said instead. As my message sank in, they began to ask questions, and I could tell they were taking me seriously. Within a few minutes, all three of them gave their lives to Jesus. I knew it was for real when one of them grabbed the bottle and poured the liquor down the sink.

This was the first time I shared my faith, and it was probably about as raw and unrehearsed as you could imagine. What I lacked in polish, though, I made up for in sincerity. My friends knew I meant what I said and could sense my deep concern for them. I couldn't have explained it then, but I knew I was somehow responsible for the world around me—my world, at least.

My friends were my responsibility.

YOUR CORNER OF THE WORLD

The sense of responsibility to make a difference in our sphere of influence pertains to every one of us. God loves the whole world and wants to reach every person. His plan for reaching each life relies on you and me. He gives us the privilege of sharing our faith with others so that they, too, can know his love and accept the free gift of salvation through his Son, Jesus Christ.

If this sounds overwhelming, keep in mind that our responsibility isn't to change *the* world—just to change *our* world. Because if we all change *our* world, then we will change *the* world. If we don't take our responsibility to influence the world seriously, we're in serious danger of being influenced by the world: "You must influence them; do not let them influence you!" (Jeremiah 15:19 NLT).

God has called every one of us to recognize and reach our spheres of influence. Many people believe there are two ways to interact with the world: as influencers or as noninfluencers. They assume that influence is reserved for famous people, celebrities, professional athletes, and politicians. But this isn't the case at all! We all have a sphere of influence.

One of my favorite scenes in the New Testament emphasizes how each of us carries responsibility for the other lives around us. Leading up to this scene, Paul and Silas were visiting Philippi, preaching the gospel and meeting with other believers there. One day on the street, they passed a slave girl known for telling fortunes and predicting the future. Possessed by an evil spirit, she recognized the Holy Spirit in Paul and Silas and shouted out that they were men of God there to save souls. Paul then commanded the spirit in her to depart in the name of Jesus, and it did—along with the girl's gift of fortune-telling.

Her masters were upset by this turn of events, of course, because of the resulting financial loss. When they found out Paul and Silas were responsible, they went to the authorities, accused them of making trouble, and had them flogged and arrested. So that's where we find these two men of God, beaten and bruised, in stocks and chains, when the most remarkable thing happens:

> Around midnight Paul and Silas were praying and singing hymns to God, and the other prisoners were listening. Suddenly, there was a massive earthquake, and the prison was shaken to its foundations. All the doors immediately flew open, and the chains of every prisoner fell off! The jailer woke up to see the prison doors wide open. He assumed the prisoners had escaped, so he drew his sword to kill himself. But Paul shouted to him, "Stop! Don't kill yourself! We are all here!"
>
> The jailer called for lights and ran to the dungeon and fell down trembling before Paul and Silas. Then he brought them out and asked, "Sirs, what must I do to be saved?"
>
> They replied, "Believe in the Lord Jesus and you will be saved, along with everyone in your household." And they shared the word of the Lord with him and with all who lived in his household. Even at that hour of the night, the jailer cared for them and washed their wounds. Then he and everyone in his household

were immediately baptized. He brought them into his house and set a meal before them, and he and his entire household rejoiced because they all believed in God. (Acts 16:25–34 NLT)

This amazing scene stands out for many reasons, but one of them stems from the use of the word translated above as "household." From the Greek word *oikos*, it literally refers to anyone under your relational roof, not just family members where you live. It's another way of describing a person's sphere of influence. As a result, this passage takes on even greater meaning for us today as we consider that when you believe in Jesus as Lord, not only will you be saved, but you will also have a profound impact on all others you influence.

CHANGE RIPPLES

The key to changing your world is first to recognize the boundaries of your sphere of influence. Most people's spheres are greater than they realize. Every day you encounter dozens of people, many on a regular basis, whom you impact one way or another. Recognizing the opportunities you have to influence them is the place to start: "Make a careful exploration of who you are and the work you have been given, and then sink yourself into that" (Galatians 6:4 THE MESSAGE). Each change you make in one area ripples into other areas. Consider some of the facets of your sphere of influence and how you can use them to share your faith.

YOUR PEOPLE

Start with the people with whom you already have close relationships—family, relatives, and close friends. Depending on your current season of life, you may also want to consider classmates, coworkers, and neighbors. "Go home to your family and tell them how much the Lord has done for you and how he has had mercy on you" (Mark 5:19 NCV).

While it may seem obvious to start here first, it's often the hardest thing to do, because these are the people whose opinions you care about the most. But when you find yourself getting nervous about sharing, remind yourself of what is most important. Though I was terrified after getting saved to share my faith with my buddies, I pushed through the fear because I cared more about where they would spend eternity than whether they thought I was weird.

Sociologists claim every person has a circle of influence averaging a dozen people. If you want to see if this holds true for you, add up all the time you spend, face-to-face, with the same people every week. If it adds up to an hour or more over the entire week, then they're in your circle. Use your ongoing contact with them as an opportunity to let them see what God is doing in your life.

YOUR PLACES

Wherever you are, literally and figuratively, God has called you to influence others there. Each of us is called to reach the individuals in the various areas that make up our sphere of influence. Let me illustrate some of the potential areas in your sphere by sharing a great story I heard involving a meeting between Loren Cunningham, the founder of Youth with a Mission (YWAM) and Bill Bright, the founder of Campus Crusade for Christ (now known as Cru).

In 1975 Loren was vacationing with his family in Colorado when he heard that Bill was visiting the same area where they were staying. Loren contacted Bill, and the two agreed to meet for lunch the next day. That night, however, Loren received a message from God to share with Bill at their meeting.

The message was clear enough. God had revealed to Loren seven areas of influence, or seven mind-molders in society, that they should think of as they pursued ministry. Whoever had the most influence in these seven areas would influence the culture, and whoever influenced the culture would make an impact on the entire nation! Knowing their shared passion for reaching young people with the message of the gospel, Loren couldn't wait to share his revelation with Bill.

The next day at lunch, after greeting one another, Loren said, "I have a word for you from the Lord." Bill looked at him with wide eyes, smiled, and said, "I have a word from God for you too!" Each then shared their message with the other, only to discover they were virtually identical. God had revealed the same seven areas of influence to both, uniting their kingdom passion for an even greater impact than they were already making individually.[1]

Both organizations have certainly made a huge difference in the lives of millions since their founders met over lunch that day. But the seven areas God revealed to them are equally important for you and me to consider today. Not every one will apply, perhaps, but I suspect most of them are already areas of your life ripe for your influence.

1. CHURCH

You may be surprised how many people overlook their local church as a place where they wield influence. But by actively participating, serving, and leading, you have a major impact on other members of the body of believers, as well as visitors and seekers. We've already discussed the importance of uniting with a strong, Bible-based church and contributing your time, talent, and treasure. But don't overlook opportunities to make sure others at your church know Jesus personally. And don't miss out on the blessing of serving them as only you can.

2. GOVERNMENT

This area includes all leaders, elected and appointed, at all levels—local, state, regional, and national. It also includes those with civil authority, such as law enforcement and the military. Many people believe the church should stay out of politics. They believe the separation of church and state must be upheld. They don't realize, however, that this separation was created to keep the government out of the church—not the church out of the government! Whether staying informed on issues and candidates, volunteering to serve as needed, running for office, or leading in a position of authority, use your influence to draw others to Christ.

3. ARTS AND ENTERTAINMENT

Arts, music, sports, fashion, and entertainment have an enormous influence on us every day. This area may appear to be so compromised and infiltrated by the enemy that you're tempted to separate yourself entirely. But some of us are called to influence this area as agents of change and catalysts for redemption. Be careful what you allow into your mind, heart, and home, but if God opens doorways, don't be afraid to use your imagination to reclaim the arts for Christ.

4. EDUCATION

Schools and educational institutions shape the minds and hearts of so many children, teens, and young adults. From daycare and preschool to elementary, junior high, high school, and college, the educational field presents frequent, ongoing opportunities to point students and teachers back to God. Unfortunately, many schools and universities that were once Christian institutions have eroded into secular melting pots of popular culture. Before we lose another generation, let's shine the light of Christ's love inside every classroom, studio, lab, and training center.

5. BUSINESS

Businesses—whether big or small, corporate or startups—remain powerful places to influence others. It's no secret that the allure of money has corrupted many businesses and clouded the moral judgment of many CEOs. More than ever, we need Christ-centered leaders willing to do their jobs and run their businesses according to the example of Christ and the Word of God. The resulting impact, not only on employees, but also on customers and the public at large, remains enormous.

6. MEDIA

The reach of the media, particularly social media, continues to grow in our culture. With countless websites, cable channels, streaming services, magazines and news sources, radio and podcasts, and various other media outlets, this area needs a major overhaul so that its vast power can be harnessed to win souls and not just sell products or promote causes or individual agendas. We need gifted, creative, Christ-led writers, editors, journalists, broadcasters, speakers, and web gurus now more than ever.

Don't criticize or condemn any form of media without first considering how you can change it for God's purposes.

7. FAMILY

Family is a social network of relationships created by God. Immediate family includes parents and their children and usually extends to include grandparents, aunts and uncles, cousins, and other relatives. God established families to be the moral center and structural pillars of a healthy society. When family order disintegrates, social order also disintegrates. Societal ills and dysfunctions can be traced to the breakdown of the family unit. Broken homes are a major contributor to almost every societal ill imaginable.

Forgive me if I seem to be making a sweeping generalization here. No one has a perfect family, nor should we try. We are called to love others like Jesus loves us. Our families provide the most practical—yet often the most challenging—areas in which to share his love. When we don't love and obey God at home, the effects ripple into all other areas. Similarly, when we do, we're able to influence not only our families, but entire neighborhoods, communities, and cities for Christ.

YOUR PASSION

We've looked at people and places where we tend to wield the most influence. But there's one more category we should keep in mind: influence related to what we're most passionate about. God gives each of us certain issues, events, people, and places that ignite our passion. Often, these passions intersect with our purpose, our talents, our circumstances, and our opportunities.

Sometimes our passions leap out at us, while other times we find ourselves searching for them. In either case, God often speaks to us through our dreams to fan the sparks of our heart's deepest longings. We see this when God poured out his Spirit on the early church, fueling a generation who saw what God sees: "Your sons and daughters will prophesy, your young men will see visions, your old men will dream dreams" (Acts 2:17).

Dreams give your faith a target. They give your faith direction and dimension. "Faith is the substance of things hoped for, the evidence of things not seen" (Hebrews 11:1 NKJV). You don't have faith if you're not hoping for something! If you're not pursuing a dream, then you're not exercising your faith. The two go hand in hand.

I believe God wants to reveal his plan for your life. Maybe he already has, and you just need to act on it by taking the next step. Or maybe you're earnestly searching and simply waiting on him to guide you. Regardless of where you are, trust that God is for you and wants to use you in powerful, purposeful, passionate ways.

Get close to him and let him stir the dreams inside you. Let his Spirit show you great things—things that are impossible in your own power but easy for God! Remember his words: "Call to Me, and I will answer you, and show you great and mighty things, which you do not know" (Jeremiah 33:3 NKJV).

YOUR NEXT STEP ON
THE JOURNEY

How do you get a dream from God? And after you have one, how do you bring it to life? I'm convinced the answers can be found in a passage written by the prophet Habakkuk in the Old Testament. Around 700 BC, during one of Israel's darkest hours, Habakkuk questioned God, crying out, "Why do the wicked prevail? Why don't you do something?"

In a classic example reminding us to be careful what we ask for, God responded by telling Habakkuk, "*You're* the solution—and I'll reveal how you will do it!" Eager and willing to participate in God's plan, Habakkuk wrote:

> I will stand at my watch and station myself on the ramparts; I will look to see what [the LORD] will say to me. . . . Then the LORD replied: "Write down the revelation and make it plain on tablets so that a herald may run with it. For the revelation awaits an appointed time; it speaks of the end and will not prove false. Though it linger, wait for it; it will certainly come and will not delay." (Habakkuk 2:1–3)

In these three verses, I can see five easy steps to help us identify and ignite our dreams. Let's briefly look at each one.

1. GET ALONE WITH GOD.

The first step is to do like Habakkuk and commit to spending some time alone with God. The watchtower was this prophet's place to pray. You will find that taking time out of your schedule and going to a special place, somewhere without all the usual distractions and interruptions, makes a huge difference in your ability to connect with God. If you want to hear God's voice, you have to turn down the world's volume.

If ever there was a time to slow down, it's now. We are far too busy and more easily distracted by more sources than ever before. For many of us, too often we're on Facebook instead of seeking God's face. We simply have to make time for him if we expect to hear his voice. The quieter you become, the more you can hear. The more you hear from God, the better you'll know what he wants.

2. FIND A WORD FROM GOD IN HIS WORD.

Next, Habakkuk says something most unusual: "I will look to see what he will say to me" (v. 1). Although he's listening for God, the prophet turns to God's Word to receive the Lord's message. God still speaks to you and me the same way today—through the Bible. There's simply no way to describe the impact God's Word can have on revealing, igniting, and fueling your dreams. The Bible is timeless, prophetic, and powerful.

I also love how practical the Bible is, offering wisdom for every situation. I remember stressing out when my kids learned to drive, so I claimed a verse from the Psalms: "The LORD will watch over your coming and going both now and forevermore" (Psalm 121:8). Similarly, when I need courage for spiritual battles, I turn to 1 John 4:4, Luke 10:19, or Romans 8:37. When I need a boost in confidence, I go to 2 Corinthians 3:6. If finances are bugging me, passages such as Philippians 4:19 and Psalm 1:1–3 give me comfort. Even when I have a toothache, I know just where to turn, my dentist's favorite verse: "Open wide your mouth and I will fill it" (Psalm 81:10).

If you want a word from God, then check out the Word of God!

3. WRITE THE DREAM.

The third phrase in the Habakkuk passage—"Write down what I reveal to you"—reminds us that recording our message from God is important. Study after study has shown that highly successful people regularly write out their dreams and how they intend to go about fulfilling them. A vision and an action plan are essential to see your dream come to life.

When you're writing down your dream, keep it God-sized! Never insult the Lord by thinking on a small scale.

God-honoring dreams are audacious, culture defying, and seemingly impossible by human standards. These dreams require absolute, faithful obedience to God each step of the way.

You're now holding one of my dreams in your hand—this book! My other dream right now is that you would have a bold, crazy, extraordinary dream of your own. Knowing that you're pursuing what God has for you is a sensation like no other. When your faith intersects with God's faithfulness, you learn to trust God in new ways.

4. WAKE UP AND DO SOMETHING.

The fourth phrase reminds us that dreams require action. Dreams are wonderful, but at some point you have to wake up and do something! God will always require us to do something. Jesus told the man with the withered hand to stretch it out (Mark 3:1–6). He told the blind man to go to the pool and wash the mud from his eyes (John 9:6–7). Even when he fed more than five thousand people, Jesus had them sit on the grass in smaller groups.

Dreams are good, but faith without works is dead: "In the same way, faith by itself, if it is not accompanied by action, is dead" (James 2:17). The distance between your dreams and reality requires your action to close the gap. If you're waiting on God to do something, keep in mind he may be waiting on *you* to do something first

5. DON'T GIVE UP ON YOUR DREAM.

Finally, Habakkuk reminds us never to give up on our dream: "Though it linger, wait for it" (Habakkuk 2:3). Many times we can't see all that God is orchestrating around us. That's why faith requires us to live based on what is unseen rather than merely what we can see. Remember, faith is not only the substance of things hoped for, but also the evidence of things not seen (Hebrews 11:1). The dream is free, but the journey isn't.

You may be tired of dreaming only to hit a dead end. You may be exhausted from all you're doing and sacrificing without seeing any fruit yet. But don't give up! It takes great endurance to see a dream fulfilled. The Bible tells us, "You need to persevere so that when you have done the will of God, you will receive what he has promised" (Hebrews 10:36).

Perseverance, in fact, is crucial to your entire journey as a follower of Jesus. No matter where you are along life's path, no matter how well or how horribly your circumstances seem to be going, trust God to lead you forward. He knows the next step you need to take to grow closer to him and to move in the direction of your divinely appointed destination. Whether you're a new believer or a seasoned veteran of the faith, with God there is always a next step!

ACKNOWLEDGMENTS

Throughout my journey of faith, God has brought amazing people into my life to help me along the way. This project is no different. So many friends, ministry partners, and team members provided assistance, support, and encouragement as I completed this book. I'm so grateful for each of you.

Thank you, Tammy. You are an amazing wife and I could not do what I do without your love and support. You not only encourage me to write but you've helped me remember the details. I can't imagine sharing this adventure with anyone else!

Thank you to my friend and mentor, John Maxwell. You loved the idea for this book from the start, and I appreciate your encouragement more than I can express.

Thank you, Dudley Delffs, my writing partner, for being a part of my life and ministry. You captured my passion for this project and helped me express it on the page.

Thank you to my agent, Matt Yates. You provided encouragement, insight, and wisdom throughout this entire process. I'm so grateful for your contribution.

Thank you, Lysa Terkeurst, and the team at Proverbs 31. Your feedback, suggestions, and support made this a much better book. I feel so blessed to have you as a friend and, with your daughter married to my son, a family member.

A special thanks to the team at Thomas Nelson, your partnership continues to bless me. I'm especially grateful for my editor, Jessica Wong, and her dedication to making this book the best it can be. It's a joy to work with you.

Thank you to my incredible staff and congregation at Church of the Highlands. You were instrumental in living out the message of *What's Next?* and inspiring me to write this book. I love you all so much and love being your pastor.

Special thanks to my sister and executive assistant, Karol Hobbs. You help me in all that I do. You are one of the best gifts God ever gave to me.

Finally, I give all thanks to Jesus Christ, my Lord and Savior. I still can't believe you let me do what I do. It is an honor to lead people to know you personally, find the freedom you gave Your life for, help them discover your purpose for their life, and together make a difference for all eternity. Thank you for choosing me.

NOTES

CHAPTER 1: BAPTISM

1. "Featured Hymn: 'I Have Decided to Follow Jesus,'" *CCEL Times* (Christian Classics Ethereal Library newsletter), October 3, 2011, http://www.ccel.org/newsletter/6/10.

CHAPTER 2: PRAYER

1. Charles R. Swindoll, "Strengthening Your Grip on Prayer," Insight for Living Ministries, March 18, 2014, https://www.insight.org/resources/article-library/individual/strengthening-your-grip-on-prayer.
2. Roberts Liardon, ed., *Smith Wigglesworth on Prayer, Power, and Miracles* (Shippensburg, PA: Destiny Image, 2006), 20.
3. Rick Warren, "Forgive Because You're Forgiven," PastorRick.com, March 12, 2018, https://pastorrick.com/devotional/english/full-post/forgive-because-you-re-forgiven3.

SECTION 2: FIND FREEDOM

1. Beth Moore, *Praying God's Word: Breaking Free from Spiritual Strongholds* (Nashville: B&H Publishing Group, 2009), 2.

CHAPTER 9: GROWTH

1. W. L. Doughty, *John Wesley: Preacher* (Eugene, OR: Wipf & Stock, 2015), 181.

SECTION 4: MAKE A DIFFERENCE

1. Elizabeth Svoboda, "Hard-Wired for Giving," *Wall Street Journal*, August 31, 2013, https://www.wsj.com/articles /hardwired-for-giving-1377902081.

CHAPTER 12: IMPACT

1. "Origin of 7 Mountain Concepts and 7MKI," Christian International, http://christianinternational.com/origin -of-7-mountain-concepts-and-7mki/.

ABOUT THE AUTHOR

C hris Hodges is the founding and senior pastor of
Church of the Highlands. Under his leadership,
Church of the Highlands has launched campuses across
the state of Alabama and has grown to more than
45,000 people attending weekly. He also cofounded
the Association of Related Churches, launched a coaching
network called GROW, and serves as chancellor of
Highlands College, a two-year ministry training college.
Chris and his wife, Tammy, have five children and live in
Birmingham, Alabama.